Breaking the Hold and Raking the Gold

The Struggle of an Immigrant Boy
on the Road to the American Dream

Joseph A. Beato

Via Nove Inc.

Published by Via Nove Inc., Detroit, Michigan, USA

ISBN (softcover): 978-0-9973663-0-3
ISBN (e-book): 978-0-9973663-1-0
Library of Congress Control Number:

10 9 8 7 6 5 4 3 2 1

Book Design by Jill Ronsley, suneditwrite.com

Printed and bound in the USA

To my late parents,
my wife, Judy,
my children,
and my grandchildren

Contents

The start of my culinary career at the Hôtel du Lac,
Lake Geneva, Switzerland, age 14

Breaking the Hold
and Raking the Gold

I t was midmorning when my dad and the school prin-
cipal walked into my first grade classroom to ask my
teacher if I could be excused.

As we walked home, my dad told me that today would
be a very important day for the whole family. We met my
mom, my brother, John, and my sister, Carmela, and together we walked to the city hall in our town, Sannicandro
Di Bari, in southeastern Italy. We had a conference with
the mayor, who gave us a new last name: Beato. My dad's
first name was also changed to Giuseppe. Before that
day, our last name was Conflitto. My dad's first name was
Europeo, but his mother, father, and friends called him
Antony. Imagine the confusion to a five-year-old, who
was too young to understand all these name changes!

I was born in 1946, after World War II, and raised in
a small town of a few thousand people in the region of
Apulia in southern Italy. My mom, Domenica, and my
dad both came from very poor families. They eloped and
were married in their teens, and began to have children
very soon after. They raised six children—John, myself,
Carmela, Vito, Anna, and Theresa. In addition there were

two others who died before the six of us were born. With no jobs, no trade, and no education, my parents became dependent on the state.

My dad was born out of wedlock and raised by Giovanni and Carmine. They had a mentally handicapped child of their own named Domenico. My mom had three brothers and one sister. I was named after my mom's dad, Giuseppe Chimienti.

Growing up in a large poor family was very challenging. We had no running water and had to walk two blocks with large buckets to get water. We used that water to drink, cook, wash clothes, and bathe. We took the dirty water back to the public fountain and dumped it into the sewer system.

Keeping warm in the winter was another challenge. After my step-grandmother died, we inherited a large basement room with twelve stairs leading down to it. To the left was a large fireplace where all the cooking was done. Near the center of the room was a four-foot wooden donut, six inches high. It held a two-foot round steel bowl filled with hot charcoal. To keep warm during the winter months, we would sit around it on regular chairs, place our feet on the wooden donut, and talk to each other until bedtime. The sleeping arrangements were poor, and somewhat crowed. To the right of the stairs was a kitchen table where all ten of us ate. A large curtain stretched across the room, creating a bedroom with a single bed to the left, where my uncle slept, and a double bed to the right, which I shared with my older brother John and Grandpa Joe. The mattresses were filled with straw and had two large holes. Each morning when my mom made the beds, she reached inside to fluff the straw. Once a week, she would add DDT powder to prevent bed bugs. On the floor between the two beds was a trap door leading to a large subterranean room, where we stored wood to keep us warm for the winter.

Under the large bed was a three-gallon terra cotta pot that we used as a toilet. It had a wooden lid and a rag on the side. Each morning, my mom would empty its contents into a steel bucket. Around seven each morning, a truck stopped at each street corner and sounded an alarm, signaling all the ladies to come dump the waste. Our biggest challenge with this chain of events was to find a clean spot on the rag to wipe ourselves until my mom would wash and replace it with a clean one.

Feeding so many people in our family was a challenge for my parents. The only person who had a steady job was my uncle. He worked for a construction company. His name was Domenico, but we called him Uncle Minguch. He was about six feet tall, well built, with very curly hair, and was as strong as an ox. In addition to being slightly mentally handicapped, he had a speech impediment, mainly because his two top front teeth were so crooked and long that they extended over his bottom lip almost to the middle of his chin. He never went to a doctor or dentist. He never attended school, so he was illiterate. He did not understand money or its value. However, he liked to carry coins in his small wallet so he could buy an espresso or a latte at the bar. He frequented many different coffee bars and never spent any money, because everyone in the town loved him and someone always stepped up to pay for his drink. He was also a very special member of our family and was very much loved at home. My Dad was very protective of our uncle. Once a week he would give him a shave. My mom washed his clothes and kept him clean and fed. He never complained about the food. For a mid-morning snack, he would take a large piece of bread and few pieces of garlic or dried hot pepper to work. He never missed church on Sunday or took any days off work. He lived with us after my step-grandma died and was always in excellent health. My dad worked at odd jobs around the town and did welfare work for the city hall as was demanded by the government. At that time no welfare recipient was allowed to sit at home and collect a paycheck. Our only other income was an old age pension check that came in monthly for my Grandpa Joe, who lived with us.

My mom was a master at stretching money to make it last through the week. She baked bread once a week and stored it in a bread box. On the weekend, she would soak the remaining stale chunks in hot water, then sprinkle them with oregano and chopped tomato and top it with a little olive oil. That was our breakfast before school, or sometimes a late snack. Today, in some of the best Italian restaurants, it is served as *bruschetta* or *pancotto*, and people pay a good price for it. Back then it was survival food—now it's a luxury! In general, our meals consisted of pasta or legumes. Meat was served only on holidays. Occasionally a little pork lard was added for flavoring in the tomato sauce. Keeping us fed, clean, and in line was a major task, and my mom was actually a slave to us all. She was the main disciplinarian and rule enforcer of the house, and everybody feared and respected her.

In those days, our only recreation was soccer. Since we didn't have a back or front yard, we played in the middle of the street. We placed a rock or a piece of clothing to indicate the goal posts, and when the ball went over the sidewalk we called out of bounds. We often had to stop due to traffic or because we had broken someone's window.

When we reached age ten, we were expected to start to work on Saturday and Sunday, doing whatever the season called for: picking olives, almonds, or grapes. The money we earned from that, and a small allowance was the only way we could buy a pair of shoes.

Back then, being Catholic and having many kids was a sign of wealth. My parents always believed that upon reaching working age, the urchins would go to work and bring money home. At the time—after the war and the end of Mussolini's dictatorship—that philosophy, paired with the idea that the government would take care of people made families dependent on the government. Thus, enslavement became the norm. My dad believed in the Democratic Party because he loved the handouts he received for voting for them, all the while enjoying less work or a complete lack thereof. We remained poor, hopeless, and disillusioned. And I, like most young people my age were praying for the day that we would reach eighteen years old and be able to migrate to another country. We dreamed of seeking work in Venezuela, Switzerland, Germany, or Canada, and of course America was the biggest dream of all.

Hundreds of single men, women, and families migrated to Germany, Switzerland, and Venezuela, because it was very easy to get visas. Canada and America were the hardest because they required a family sponsor. The length of waiting periods varied, depending on the closeness of the relative that was willing to sponsor you. Most visas were granted to children, husbands, wives, brothers, and sisters, but I had only my Uncle Nick in Windsor, Ontario, Canada, Uncle Nick had moved to Canada years before on his own, later sending for his wife, and then his two children, who joined their parents after a five year waiting period. The two children lived with my family during that period, raising the family size to twelve. So the time went by and I lived my life, living and dreaming for the day when I would get a break and be able to get a visa to go some place new

Giacomo Farella was a big-time *brigante*, which means "bandit" in Italian. He stole from the rich and gave to the poor, much like Robin Hood, he was feared and loved by the people, pursued by the law, and eventually gunned down at about age fifty.

Giacomo was married to Maria, the eldest sister of my Aunt Angelina, and my grandmother Teresa. When she was fourteen, Teresa lived with Giacomo and Maria. Teresa's parents lived in New York and were in the process of filing immigration papers for her. In 1914, while Europe was at war, Giacomo raped Teresa and she became pregnant. When she gave birth, her family gave the baby to a lady named Carmine, who had recently lost a baby at birth. Carmine was thrilled to receive the healthy baby boy, who grew up to marry my mom and become my dad. For fear of retaliation from Giacomo, the rape was never reported. Instead, to cover up the pregnancy and hide their shame, Theresa's parents sent for her to

New York to join them, and left the baby in Sannicandro to be raised by Carmine.

When I was about ten years old, a man who had just returned after spending several years in America, approached my dad and, out of nowhere, gave him a letter and an American $100 bill. The letter explained that his biological mother was alive. Imagine the joy that news brought to our family!

After moving to America, Teresa went on with her life. She settled in New York, got married, and had six children. Her first legitimate child was named Tony, like my father. Teresa practiced the Pentecostal religion and, after her husband died, confessed her sin of having abandoned a child at birth, saying she did not know if he was dead or alive. The church strongly suggested that it was not too late and said she must seek the truth for her salvation. With God's help, she found the courage to write her first letter, which read, "Dear Son, if you are alive, please forgive me and write back to me. I am your biological mother." She gave the letter to a man who was returning to Italy, who in turn delivered it to my dad.

My father was aware of the circumstances of his birth. However, after many happy years of childhood and feeling loved by Carmine and without knowledge of his biological mother's whereabouts, he spent less and less time thinking about her.

Carmine raised my dad without legal papers because of the ongoing war. His name was registered as Conflitto Europeo, meaning "European Conflict," at the city hall after the war. However, Carmine named him Tony, after his biological grandfather.

During his adult life, my dad fought hard with City Hall to get his last named changed from Conflitto to his biological mother's maiden name, Beato. Finally, one very important day at city hall, my father got his wish and was awarded his new name, Giuseppe Beato.

After receiving the letter and the money from his mother, my dad immediately wrote back explaining the family's situation. He also sent a photo of each one of us and our ages. After that the communications from my grandma came often by mail, always with some money and, many times, in the form of big boxes full of clothes for everybody in the family.

That first letter written by my grandma revealing the fact that she was still alive was very special and gave us hope of the American dream. But that dream was soon shattered because Grandma acquired a different last name when she married and had left my dad behind with no paper trail to prove they were related.

My older brother, John, was the first one to leave home for Switzerland. He settled in Estavayer-le-Lac, a small town in the canton of Fribourg, He rented a two-bedroom apartment on the second floor from a very nice couple. He earned his living working as a painter. A year later, when John was well established, my dad decided to seek work and joined my brother. "Not with out me!" I insisted. Finally, I won the argument and was excited to be part of the venture to Switzerland. Because In Italy we had no money and no work, and with the same socialistic policies maintained by the Democratic Party, we had no future.

Growing up in a small town, with my parents struggling to feed the family, we often resorted to stealing olives that we would sell so we could go to a movie. Then we would see people returning to Italy for short visit, or getting married. We would be in awe as we saw them spending so much money that they now had in their pockets, money that they had earned, in their new countries and new jobs. It was especially true of those from America. I have memories of one young man returning to our town to get married. In a brand new convertible '57 Chevrolet, he paraded through the town after the church ceremony, throwing sugar-covered almonds called confetti, spearmint gum, and some American dollars into the crowd. I remember me and my friends pushing and shoving each other to pickup as many dollars as possible. These incidents only reinforced my dream to achieve the ultimate goal—to get to America.

I was only fourteen when my dad and I set out for Switzerland. I quit school in the third year of high school, a bad student who hated school. My dad told us that if we didn't do well in school, we would work as a laborer for the rest of our life. I regret not having studied now, but at the time, I chose labor.

The train to Switzerland stopped at Lugano, in the Italian region. Our destination was Lausanne, which was on the French side of the country. There we would meet my brother John at 8 p.m., and then proceed to Estavayer-le-Lac, where he lived. At 2 o'clock, we disembarked at Lugano and spent an hour going through customs. The next train was scheduled to leave at 5 p.m. and arrive in

Lausanne at 8 o'clock. Swiss trains were always on time. You could set your watch by them.

We had two hours to kill but no money to eat in a restaurant, so my dad improvised. He opened a suitcase and pulled out a dry sausage, a hunk of cheese, and some bread. We found a corner in the waiting room, sat down, and used the top of a suitcase as a table. I was so embarrassed! I guess it was typical of how any fourteen-year-old boy would feel, being watched by hundreds of people passing as you tried to eat. Lunch was over, and we still had some time to kill. My dad pulled out his wallet. He had 300 liras left, which was about two Swiss francs. I spotted some Italian playing cards in the gift shop and went to buy them, because we no longer needed Italian money. The train ticket to Lausanne had been paid in full, and I thought we would be able to play cards in the evening with my brother.

At 4:15, I was watching our luggage when my dad returned abruptly from a walk. "Hurry!" he said, in the Italian dialect specific to our town. "Another train is leaving in 10 minutes for Lausanne!" "Are you sure?" I said. My dad replied that he had asked the train attendant. Though I was skeptical, I knew everyone in Lugano spoke Italian, so I agreed. After all, travelling would be better than waiting.

The train cabin sat six people. We shared it with an older couple and a single man. After the second stop an attractive middle-aged lady joined us. Two hours later, the ticket controller came by, and everyone took out their tickets. My dad was the last. When the controller spoke to him, he turned to me and asked what he was talking about, because I had studied French for two years at school. Much to my surprise, the man spoke German and I became anxious and embarrassed. I didn't know what he wanted. The tickets had been paid for through an agency in Bari. The lady who had joined us in the cabin told the controller that she new Italian and offered to translate. That is when we discovered that we had taken the wrong train. In self-defense, my dad said that he had personally checked with a train attendant in Lugano, who assured him that this train would go to Lausanne.

Through the translation we learned that indeed our final stop would be Lausanne, but we wouldn't reach there until 1:00 a.m., because this train was taking a long route through the German part of Switzerland. My dad replied that it was all right, as long we ended up in Lausanne. After all, it was our mistake. My stomach was sick from embarrassment. The controller told the translator it would cost us eighty francs per person. My dad pleaded, saying we had no money and his older son was waiting in Lausanne, and he would pay when we arrived. The controller accepted none of this and informed the lady that he would escort us out at the next stop. With an air of arrogance, devoid of compassion, he said his decision was final.

What I saw next was nothing short of a miracle! The lady took 160 francs out of her wallet and paid the controller on our behalf. Stunned by her act of kindness and generosity, we were speechless. All we could say was thank you. We asked for her address so we could send her money back. She replied not to worry—it wasn't necessary—and wished us good luck. Two stops later, she reached her destination and left, waving good-bye.

I continued to experience the generosity of the Swiss people during my five years in Switzerland, with the exception of people in uniform, who stuck to rules with uncompromising rigidity.

At precisely 1:00 a.m., the train pulled into the Lausanne station. Tired from the long ride and lack of sleep, we managed to find a bench and arranged our luggage. We looked around for my brother, but he was nowhere in sight. Much to our surprise, nobody was there at all, nor were there any phones. We looked at the arrival board, which indicated that the next train from Lugano would arrive at 8 a.m. Assuming that my brother would return in the morning to meet that train, we made ourselves comfortable on two benches and tried to get some sleep.

Few minutes later we heard a loud whistle as a crew of men with large hoses washed down the platform. A man in uniform approached, waving at us to leave the area. Equipped with my two years of French classes at school, I asked if there was any place where we could wait until 8 o'clock. The man responded that from one to five was cleaning time and we had to leave—pronto!

January in Switzerland was not like January in southern Italy. Cold wind and snow blew in our faces as we exited the train station. We stood hopeless, waiting for our next savior, with no site of my brother, John.

Two taxis stopped and asked if we needed assistance. Knowing that we had no money, I replied, "*Non, merci.*" My dad asked me if I had my brother's address. I said yes and pulled a torn corner of an envelope out of my pocket. "The next time a taxi comes by, you show them the address and see if they can go to that town." "Why ask," I said, "if we don't have any money?" "Because there is a strong possibility that John went home, knowing that the next train would arrive in the morning," was my dad's response.

I was hopeful but not convinced. I waved at the next taxi, showed the address. Yes! He immediately loaded our luggage and we sat down in the warm car.

The last time I had seen snow was in 1956, when Southern Italy was hit by snow that immobilized Sannicandro Di Bari. The city employed many men with shovels and pick-up trucks to transport the snow to the outskirts of the city. I remember skimming the snow from the top and running into the house with it. My mom would add sugar and fresh lemon juice, making it into a sorbet or lemon slush. It was such fun!

This time was different. I was traveling in the back seat of a taxi trough the mountains, worrying about whether my brother would be home to pay the fare. Sleep-deprived and with a knot in my stomach, I looked out the window as we arrived at our destination.

My dad exited the taxi and walked to the trunk of the car to unload the luggage. The driver gestured: money first or no luggage! I matched the house number with the address on the paper and knocked on the door several times Dogs started to bark, waking people up, who called out from different balconies. One was a member of the family where my brother was staying. The taxi driver explained the situation and his requirement: payment for his work before he released the luggage. Within a few minutes, the lady appeared downstairs, paid the driver, helped us with the luggage, and escorted us to our room.

She said my brother was still in Lausanne in a motel for the night. "There is no need to worry," she said. "See you at breakfast."

Finally safe, warm, and out of the cold bitter night, once again the Swiss people had come to our rescue with great compassion. Sleeping didn't come easy, but at last we got some rest.

The next day my brother gave up waiting when we didn't show up on the 8 a.m. train. By eleven o'clock he was home and overjoyed to see us. He repaid the landlady for the taxi and I told him about my first experience travelling out of my home country.

Estavayer-le-Lac was a small town of a few thousand people, with streets made of cobblestones. There was a milk factory *(latterrie)*, five small hotels, each with a restaurant and bar, a fishery, the beautiful stone Gothic Abbey church, two bakeries *(boulangerie)*, and a large 12th-century castle, the Château de Chenaux, occupied by the police department. A tea room, which served pastries, coffee, tea, and adult beverages, became my hangout on my days off. Within a quarter of a mile was Lake Geneva, with a long pier and a beautiful resort hotel called Hôtel du Lac.

For two days, my dad and I tried to get working permits from the police department. I was the translator, and I managed well with the French I had learned in school, only to find out that I was too young to get a permit to work anywhere unless a Swiss family would assume responsibility for me—and the only options were hotel or farm work. I chose the hotel.

Mr. and Mrs. Torche, the owners of the Hôtel du Lac resort, sponsored my work permit. I was very happy and agreed to a salary of 250 Swiss francs per month (about 65 dollars) plus room and board. I would eat at the hotel and share a two-bedroom boathouse nearby with a Spanish boy named Julio. We were both *garçons de maison,* which meant we did general housework.

It was a three-story hotel with twenty-four rooms. Balconies faced the lake with a stunning view, and a three-level brick patio descended to the water's edge. On the first floor was an L-shaped bar with six bar stools, tables, and chairs for about fifty people. Connected to it was a long, narrow dining room that seated about a hundred and twenty people, and was elegantly decorated in a marine motif. Windows looked out across the lake. Beside the front door on the street level was a small but compact and well-equipped two-level kitchen. The window was so large that it looked out on the street, as well as the pier.

Work started at 7:00 a.m. on the third floor. We cleaned and vacuumed the hallway carpets, washed three sets of stairs because there was no elevator, cleaned the bathrooms and the bar area—all by 11:30. Chef Hans Stoesel, a Swiss-German from Zurich, and his kitchen staff started at 8:30, while the bartender and dining room staff began at 9:00. The waiters had until 11:30 to vacuum the dining room, set the tables with starched tablecloths, polish water and wine glasses, and place a fresh flower in each stem vase. Madame Boudoix and a helper ran the laundry room, washing all the linens, towels, sheets, and serviettes, as well as my personal clothing. Mr. and Mrs. Torche arrived at 10:00 every morning, and after a short visit with each employee, went to their office. The *maitre d'hotel* arrived at 11:00, inspected the dining room, reviewed all the reservations, and inspected the waiters' appearance and apparel. Everyone was in full uniform, starched and clean. At precisely 11:30 everybody sat down at one table and ate like a big family. At noon, the dining room opened for service. My duty was to clear the large table and take over a three-basin sink to wash dishes, silverware, pots and pans, and do everything else the chef might command, such as peeling potatoes and rinsing vegetables. Though the kitchen was hot and smoky and we were hot and sweaty, the service ran smoothly. Nobody was allowed to speak—only the chef called orders and the assistants replied: "Yes, Chef!" "No, Chef!" This went on until 2:00 p.m. sharp. Then the dining service ended, the chef went home, and the kitchen staff started cleaning the stoves and kitchen equipment. They went home an hour later.

My job was to finish the dishes and mop the floor before going home to my little chalet at 3:30. I would return to duty two hours later. The chef and all other staff were back at 5:00. The whole staff sat down together at 5:30 to eat dinner.

The most difficult job was that of the sous-chef that the chef appointed to cook for the staff. He had to watch food costs because the owner ate with us. He had to keep the staff happy. He had a free hand to be creative, and he was most often the one that took any criticism. Dinner service went from 6:00 to 9:00 p.m. Then the chef left and the rest of us cleaned up. I was the last one to leave, usually at 10:30. Each day the routine was the same, except for my one day off, usually Monday. Working six days a week for long hours, I looked forward to my day off to do what I wanted—mostly visit my dad.

Chef Hans seemed to like me. After a few months on the job, he advanced me to different stations, frequently with minor cooking duties, such as breading, assembling cold platters, making dressings, and peeling potatoes. I loved my job. Finally I was working on my own! And at the end of every month I got paid. The money was sent back to my family, who were badly in need. I loved the idea that I was contributing, and not depending on the government to buy food and clothes. I loved that my dad let me keep a small portion of my earnings to spend as I pleased. I loved when my mom would send pictures of new clothes she had bought for herself and the rest of the family. Above all, I loved learning a new trade and I was gaining so much satisfaction from it. One day, the chef said I would make a good cook and that I should ask my dad if I could join an apprenticeship program. My dad agreed without hesitation. For the next three years, I was a chef apprentice.

Learning French came easy for me; nevertheless, I worked hard at it every afternoon in my cabin. I read different magazines, and I listened to songs on my 45-record player over and over, sung by my favorites singers like Johnny Hallyday, Sylvie Vartan, and Françoise Hardy. Listening to these singers enhanced my further learning of the French language. I also listened to my very favorite American singer, my idol, Elvis Presley, as well as a few

Italian singers like Adriano Celentano, Little Tony, and Rita Pavone. Learning other languages was easy because the hotel kitchen was a melting pot of Italian, German, French, and Spanish employees, who often translated words from one language to the other.

The next three years of apprenticeship under Chef Hans were hard. He was old school, and he demanded perfection in every dish that I made. His motto was "Either learn—or get out of the kitchen or the apprenticeship program!" He never allowed me to question his authority or instructions, especially during lunch or dinner service. I could only say, "Yes, Chef!" or "No, Chef!"

Chef Hans pulled me into his office one day after lunch I knew it was time for discipline. But to my surprise, he went to the bar, poured two cold glasses of beer, we toasted. Then he placed a blank piece of white paper on the table and asked me what color it was. I replied that it was white. He stated that it was red and told me to take a second look. Again, I replied that it was white. That was when he made me fully understand that during service, if he said it was red, so be it with no talking back. I understood that if everybody talked back at the chef there would be chaos and an atmosphere of disrespect in the kitchen. With that understood, we finished our beer. Before we separated, he told me once again that I was doing a great job.

From December 1 to January 15, the hotel closed for the holidays. What a great chance for me to travel back home to spend the holidays with my family, away from the cold weather! But this time, with the help of Swiss francs, everything would be much better than on previous holidays. What a simple concept: by providing me with a job, I was provided with happiness, dignity, success, and self respect. My dad and my brother returned to Italy after two years in Switzerland. My brother opened a business painting doors, houses, and other buildings, and he did well. My dad helped my brother and continued his correspondence with Grandma in New York.

When I finished my three-year apprenticeship, Mr. Torche offered me an opportunity: for two more years. I would be in charge of the kitchen as chef during the months of September to December. What a great deal of responsibility was bestowed on me! But I managed well and earned more money, and my boss was happy.

One major event that I will never forget happened one late afternoon while I was having a drink with my friends in the tea room, the jukebox was playing a Jonny Halliday song when the owner abruptly unplugged the jukebox and announced that President Kennedy had been shot and was dead on arrival at the hospital. Before she could finish the sentence she was in tears. Not one word was spoken. The news was like a stab in the heart of each one of us. We sat with long faces and fear of what would come next, discussing among ourselves who would commit such a barbarian act. I witnessed just how much John Kennedy was respected and loved around the world, especially in Switzerland.

After my eighteenth birthday, I wrote from Switzerland to my Uncle Nick in Canada and asked him if he could find me a restaurant that would sponsor me to immigrate to Canada, offering me employment as a specialized cook. That would enable me to submit my application at the Canadian embassy in Bern. My uncle told me that it would be difficult to get a visa that way. I responded that I had nothing to lose and that was the only way to break through the red tape and immigrate as a professional, because we had no immediate family to sponsor us.

Two weeks later I received a letter from my Uncle Nick with two affidavits—one from my uncle stating that upon arrival in Canada he would give me room and board and assume all responsibility for me, and the other from the owner of a restaurant, Vito's Cave, in London, Ontario, guaranteeing me work upon arrival. On my next day off, which was a Monday morning; I took the train to Bern and went to the Canadian embassy. I filled out all the necessary papers, and was assured that the application would be processed but there were no guaranties.

Riding the train back home, I had many thoughts: What if I were to be the first person to break through? What if they rejected my application? That would be a great disappointment. Would I try a different angle? Or maybe my uncle was right—it was too difficult if you didn't have immediate family in Canada. On the other hand, I was happy with my job, I was well-liked, and I could continue to have a good career in Switzerland.

Mr. and Mrs. Torche were stunned when I mentioned the possibility that I might immigrate to Canada. They wished me the best, although I don't think that they thought it would ever become a reality. I assured them if my papers came through, I would stay at the hotel through the summer and depart in the fall, after the busy season. I decided not to dwell on the issue too much and told my parents that they should not hold out a lot of hope.

July came and went. So did August. All my hopes were fading away.

When I opened the registered letter from the embassy the first week in September, my stomach was in knots. With great anxiety, I read the letter. It was informing me that my application had been accepted and I should appear for an interview at the embassy at 10:00 a.m. three days later. Happiness was an understatement! I shared the news with the kitchen staff and my boss, who all said they were happy for me, but they would be sad to lose me. After an intense interview at the embassy, I received my visa welcoming me to Canada.

For the next three weeks I was on cloud nine. My co-workers teased me, saying I would not like Canada and I would be back within six months, begging to get my job back. I responded by saying the next time you see me in Switzerland, my face will be on the dollar bill!

I saved money by skimming from what I had been sending home for the family in order to purchase a seat on the SS Olympia that was to leave for Canada on October 14, 1964. It was a sad day when I said goodbye to the Swiss family I had become so attached to. But I had a major goal to attain and my whole life lay ahead of me to live and explore. I was only eighteen years old and starting a whole new chapter in my life.

The last two weeks with my family was somewhat somber. My mom and my grandpa especially, were worried that I was too young to travel so far. My mother cried every day reliving a past experience from her childhood. When she was a little girl, my grandpa sent his oldest son, Vito, my mother's older brother, to Argentina to look for work. He wrote back a couple of times and then vanished without a trace. When I was ready to leave for Canada, Grandpa was eighty-seven years old. He told me that if I left, he would probably never see me again. I replied that this was nonsense, I loved him, and I would definitely see him soon. The rest of my family was very happy for me because it meant breaking through the hold and getting a chance to reach my dream.

When we arrived at the port of Naples I glanced at the Olympia. The ship was the size of my town—so huge, so impressive to look at, decorated with every flag in the world and multicolor banners. A live band was playing loud music, with the captain and crew nearby, dressed in white uniforms. As we walked on board, families and friends of the passengers were waving handkerchiefs in the air; many of them crying, others yelling and laughing. It was just spectacular as we slowly moved away from the port, watching people continue to wave in the distance until it all faded away.

In order to get to my destination in Windsor, Ontario, Canada, the ship navigated rough waters for nine days. The SS Olympia was built in 1953 for the Greek Line (General Steam Navigation Company of Greece) for transatlantic voyages. It operated well, though without the luxury of the Andrea Doria or the Michelangelo. It was all I could afford, and as long as it got me to Canada safe, I was happy. I made a few friends on board, some my age and others slightly older. I shared a cabin with six others in the economy class at the very bottom of the vessel,. It had small, thick, oval windows that allowed us to see only water as we travelled. The dining room was huge. The food was good and we could eat as much as we wanted. At night we had a choice of listening to live music, dancing, cinema, or just relaxing wherever we wished.

I spent many hours relaxing and reflecting on where I was headed after so many years watching my family struggle. At times it had seemed like life was on hold and we could not advance. We were stuck, always dependent on the social conditions of the government, which never provided work, but instead, assistance so that they could manipulate people and dictate how far we could get in life. The government enslaved people with what they called goodwill. They wanted us to feel we needed them, giving the big promise that they would take care of us because we were not capable on our own. Election time was a contest of who would offer the most, whether the Democratic Party, the Communist Party, or the Party of Monarchist Unity, but they never gave money—always olives, flour, oil, wine, or dried legumes—all the same with the same goal of enslavement. I never had a sense of achievement until I went to Switzerland and learned that a simple job and working hard could solve many problems including that of self-esteem. I resolved to work hard on the long journey ahead, and with the help of God and family I would be successful.

After nine long days we arrived in Halifax, Nova Scotia, on the east coast of Canada. We waited there for six hours and then boarded our train to Toronto, Ontario. From Toronto, we would proceed to Windsor, a trip that seemed to take forever. Four of my friends from the Olympia had tickets for the same train to Toronto. Three were staying there, and one was going to London, Ontario. We decided to get a bite to eat at a tavern-restaurant-bar near the port. Upon entering, we noticed two large rooms—one for men only and one for men and women. We sat at a round table and asked the waiter if he spoke Italian or French. He said yes to French. So I ordered a round of beer on tap and hot chicken sandwiches for everybody. I was just about to order another round when the waiter decided to check our IDs. I was the only one who was eighteen. The waiter informed me that I was a minor and it was against the law for me even to enter a tavern. At first, I thought the guy was joking, but he explained to us:" Welcome to Canada, it's the law of the land". We were very surprised, because there was no such law in Europe. We ate fast and left.

After the long train ride to Windsor, I finally met my Uncle Nick, who was waiting for me at the station. I was so happy to reunite with my relatives! I shared a bedroom with my two cousins, Joe and Ricky. The youngest was eight years old and born in Canada, but he spoke perfect Italian. Everywhere we went, he loved to translate English for me. The first time we took a walk in town, he took me down the river, and there it was—America! Detroit, Michigan! Only the river separated the two countries. The big, tall buildings were so close that I could almost touch them, and my uncle promised me that as soon as I learned English and found a job, I would be able to apply for a visitor's visa.

I tried to get a job at the well known Prince Edward Hotel and the Embassy Hotel, but since I didn't speak English, they could not hire me. I settled for a job that paid one dollar an hour at the Volcano Pizzeria, where everyone spoke Italian, I was off on Mondays, so I enrolled in a Monday night adult education class tailored for immigrants who needed to learn English. With that and the help I got from my little cousin, I soon started to speak broken English. I knew that I was well aware that my handle on the English language was the key to getting a good job in my field. Within four months I was doing quite well.

Across from the pizzeria where working was a night club called Killarney Supper Club. One day, I mustered my courage, walked into the kitchen through the back door, and asked to see the chef. Ahty Amaleinen, a Swedish chef educated in France, after a brief interview offered me a job for four dollars per hour. I told him that I would not let him down, and I didn't. I worked for him for the next two years and gained so much knowledge from him. The next job I got was executive chef in an upscale Italian restaurant, Gino's Italian Village. I was determined to do a good job and make money for the owner. I worked hard to balance food quality, personnel, and food costs.

My next step up was taking a chef certification test that required a score of 75% to pass, and I scored 97%. I made my relatives proud, and my pay kept increasing enabling me to send more money to my family in Italy. During the five years I spent in Canada, I managed to file the appropriate immigration papers for my older brother and sister to come to Canada, both of whom came and found good jobs.

While working as executive chef at Gino's Italian Village, I convinced my boss, Gino, to sponsor one of my best friends in Sannicandro Di Bari so he could immigrate to Canada. On my last visit to Italy, Tony De Pinto, who had been working as an electrician for his dad, begged me to help him find a way to Canada. Due to the lack of work at home, both of his parents pleaded with me to help their son, the oldest of their six children, as they were desperately in need. The only people I knew in Canada were restaurant owners—no one in the electrical business. So I brainstormed the possibility of Tony getting a letter from a couple of restaurants in Italy, stating that he was a cook and had worked in their establishments for few years,. Meanwhile, I convinced my boss that I would be completely responsible for him if and when he arrived in Canada, just as my Uncle Nick had done for me five years earlier. I told Tony that it was a long shot because we where not related, but after a hopeful, year-long wait, Tony got his working visa and joined me in Canada.

I found him a place to stay with two single guys, sharing the rent of a three-bedroom house, and hired him at the restaurant I worked at. He started the same way I did in Switzerland—washing dishes and cleaning carpets. My boss, Gino, loved him, and so did the rest of the staff. Tony earned just enough money to pay his rent while learning English. After a few months, he found employment installing electrical systems in mobile trailers built by a large company called Pyramid. He worked under the supervision of an electrician for the next two years before taking a test and becoming a licensed electrician himself. Tony and I became like brothers, and he was honored to be the best man at my wedding. I met my wife to be on a blind date arranged by my brother's wife. My brother John was already in the United States. We went to dinner and dancing. We went to a Detroit Tiger baseball game that summer. She wanted me to witness the great American game of baseball. I really wasn't impressed and fell asleep during the game. The rest is history. We were married in 1970.

Judy was born on March 9, 1947, in Detroit. Her parents, Gordon and Dorothy, were born in Ottawa, Canada, and she had a sister, Gloria, whose husband, Duane Belanger, worked for the Detroit News. Judy graduated from the Grace Hospital School of Nursing in 1969. We lived in a tiny 3 room apartment, before buying our first house in Detroit. My son, Robert, was born in 1972, and my daughter, Kelli, eighteen months later in 1974.

Soon after our wedding, my friend Tony was transferred to Coburg, Ontario, a small town on Lake Ontario. He loved his new home because it was surrounded by lakes and streams, which satisfied his passion for fishing. He married a beautiful girl named Margaret, and they had two children named Claudia and Stephan. We visited each other at least once a year. My family's best memories are of the days we spent fishing on Rice Lake with Tony and Margaret and their family. Tony and I also spent many vacation nights with our sons on the shores of Lake Ontario, fishing, sitting around a bonfire, and drinking a gallon of homemade wine until the early hours of the morning. Life was good.

Yes, life was good—but unpredictable. About twenty years later, I suffered a big blow. Tony, became hill with cancer. After surgery and many rounds of intense radiation, we received good news. His cancer was in remission. We attended his daughter's wedding and Tony looked well. He had beaten the cancer and was optimistic for continued health. However, a few months later, the cancer returned with a vengeance. Soon afterwards, I lost my best friend. He was only in his early fifties. It was devastating to me. I was left with only memories of our many happy memories and the many adventures we had. These cherished memories are the subject of much laughter as they are relived over and over again, when I visit with his family.

In 1967, I watched Detroit burn from riots due to race relations. Governor Romney sent army troops into the city, and together with the police department, they restored order. But the riots lasted seven days while the world watched. I could not understand the reason that people destroyed other people's properties. Surely, I thought, there must be other ways to demonstrate. At the same time, I felt sorry for the oppressed and for everyone who got hurt. It was a black eye for America. Properties were not repaired and remained dilapidated for many years after the riots subsided. Store owners moved their businesses to the suburbs, and the population in the city kept decreasing. Within a year, Detroit showed resilience and started to come back, especially in the fall of 1968, when the Detroit Tigers won the World Series. My interest in baseball had grown somewhat after that first game. However soccer was my first love. It was the game; I grew up playing, and continued to love. After spending years in Canada, I must admit, I had become very interested in hockey.

I filed with US immigration to get a working visa in 1970. Within a few months, we had put a little money down on a small two-bedroom home on the east side of Detroit. Soon after that, I received my green card and I could legally work in America. My dream had become a waking realty—the dream I had waited so long to fulfill. Judy and I spent a two-month honeymoon in Italy, in 1971. We visited the rest of my family and the area surrounding Sannicandro Di Bari, and we travelled to Naples, Rome, Venice, Pisa, the Isle of Capri, Sorrento, and Florence. We also took a trip to Switzerland and spent a few days at the Hôtel du Lac, where I had done my chef's apprenticeship, visiting my old bosses, Mr. and Mrs. Torche. I praised America everywhere I went. Life was good, and I had made my parents proud.

Upon returning from our trip to Italy, I got a job as a cook in an Italian restaurant, where I worked for few months. I was very happy that both Judy and I were working. She worked in various nursing homes and hospitals that were lenient with her schedule. This was helpful when we had young children. But before long, I craved a greater challenge and decided to take a job as executive chef at the Oakwood Hospital and Medical Center in Dearborn, Michigan. I worked closely with dieticians and learned a lot about different diets—a field of which I knew very little—such as what food was needed for different illnesses. That took me back to when I was sick as a child and the doctor would recommend what food to eat so I would get better. It was usually more expensive food, such as eggs and meat, food that my parents struggled to buy. Working in health care was very interesting and challenging. Once I had mastered the concepts of different diets and knew what a patient could or not have, I began to develop my own recipes and introduced new dishes.

* * *

One day in 1972 I received a phone call from my Godfather in Italy informing me that he was coming to America to visit relatives in New York. I took the opportunity to go there, and I brought him back to Detroit to visit us for couple of days. While I was in New York, I searched through the phone book to see if I could find my grandma's number. After a few tries, she answered! When I said, "Hi Grandma," she froze. A few seconds later, she asked me how I had got her number and whether I was in New York. I replied, "Yes, I am here, with a great desire to meet you." She became very nervous and told me not to come and not to call anymore, because it would be dangerous for her, and that one day I would understand the situation. The she hung up.

Feeling rejected, I wrote a letter to my dad, explaining the event. Two weeks later, he wrote me back, apologizing on Grandma's behalf and informing me that she had acted that way because all her children's didn't know anything about her past and she would reveal it in time.

Meanwhile my brother, John, was filing American immigration papers for the rest of our family in Italy. After a long period of waiting and many hours at the immigration office in Detroit, they received their visas and came to America. That came with a big sacrifice, especially for my dad, who had to leave his stepbrother, Uncle Minguch, behind in a nursing home in Italy because he had a different last name. We spent a lot of money on attorney fees and presented a compassion case to local politicians guaranteeing that we would comply with all responsibilities for him to get permission to come to America. Finally, all roads came to an end. It was truly heartbreaking, because we were so attached to him. We knew his life-long hard work had benefitted all of us, because he never knew the value of money and on payday he would give all his money to my mom. He had lived a happy life with us, and he died at age seventy-nine while my dad was there visiting.

My parents settled on the east side of Detroit in a three-bedroom bungalow with my two younger sisters, Anna and Theresa, both of whom finished high school and later married. My dad worked with my brother John, as a painter. A few months after settling in Detroit, he visited his mother in New York and pressured her to tell the rest of the family her story and reunite with him. With the help of the church, she finally broke her silence.

She told her oldest son, Tony, first. Then she gathered him and her other five children together and broke her story to them. "Remember when I used to collect your outgrown clothes when you were children and young adults, and or when I would ask for five, ten, or twenty dollars from each of you? I always used the excuse that I was donating to the church, but in fact I was sending everything to a needy family in Italy It was the family of the son that I left behind long ago when I came to America. "You have a step brother in Italy, and I have been sending packages to him and his family." She asked for their understanding regarding what had happened when she was a young girl in Italy and begged their forgiveness for having kept her secret for so long. With shock, surprise, and understanding they all forgave her and, in fact, were anxious to meet our family. They welcomed my dad and all of us with much celebration.

A date was set for the reunion. My Grandma flew from New York with her oldest son Tony. My brother John picked them up from the airport. When they arrived home, my brother in law, Duane Belanger, who worked for the Detroit News as a photographer, covered the reunion at my dad's house, and the story got a full page in the paper.

I missed the initial reunion because of work. After work I drove to my dad's house to finally meet them, and I was shocked to see the resemblance of both grandma and Uncle Tony to the rest of the family. Tony was practically identical to my dad, and I felt that I had known them all my life. That reunion was truly a major accomplishment. They stayed for two weeks with my parents before returning to New York.

Soon after, we learned that my Grandma's sister, Angelina, wanted to come to Detroit with her son, Don Antonio, my father's first cousin. He was a priest in the main church we had frequented as children, called Chiesa Madre. We raised money in America to buy a new organ for the church. I organized a fund-raiser dinner-dance, rented a hall, cooked for about 150 people and raised a few thousand dollars. We made sure that Grandma and Uncle Tony from New York were present for the occasion, most importantly because it was to be a reunion for my Grandma and her sister Angelina who hadn't seen each other since childhood During Angelina and Don Antonio's two-week stay at my parents' house, we had many conversations on many subjects while relaxing, having dinner, and drinking wine. My dad wanted an answer to his life long question. He had always been plagued by the question as to why Grandma had waited so long to try and find him. The answer was simple, but shocking.

My grandmother's parents had owned some land and property in Italy. When they died, the land was to be divided in equal parts between the three sisters. By then, the oldest sister, Maria, had died, My Grandma, was of course, married and living in America Angelina was the only sister living in Italy. She was the only person still communicating with Grandma. One day, Grandma received a legal document to sign. It stated that if she signed it, she would be signing over her portion of the inheritance. Angelina told her sister, that since she was living the good life in America, she no longer needed that part of her inheritance. Grandma did not sign, but replied that she could not do that because she had a son that she wanted to give it to. Angelina wrote a letter in reply, stating that the boy Grandma had left behind in Italy hadn't survived. He had passed away, and Angelina, not wanting to upset her sister, chose to not inform her of the death. After hearing that heart breaking news, Grandma signed the document.

Some 50 years later at the reunion of the two sisters, Angelina begged for forgiveness.

Many years after Grandma received the news of her son's death, she began to have some doubts about the story, as she heard a visitor from her town talking about a family in Sannicandro. The story seemed to fit the narrative of her situation. She began investigating, and discovered that, yes, her son was alive. Little by little, she gained courage, and combining that with her faith, she did the right thing. She lived for another ten years, frequently visiting and talking on the phone with my mom and dad and the rest of our family. I like to believe that she died in peace.

* * *

I continued to work at Oakwood Hospital (which later became a multi-branched medical center) for five years running a smooth operation, improving food quality, controlling food and labor costs, and being well-liked by the administration and physicians. We moved to a bigger house in the suburbs and our first boy, Robert Antony, was born August 5, 1972. Our daughter, Kelli Ann was born March 10, 1974. Life was good.

Ben Schwartz, a head hunter, owned a job recruitment agency in Detroit. He specialized in placing executives in the food business. Early one evening in 1975, I received a phone call from Ben. He asked me if I would be willing to make a move and take a greater challenge. At that time, the Henry Ford Hospital had 1200 beds, while Oakwood had just 600. Moreover, it was a teaching hospital for doctors, nurses, and dietetic interns. It had one large central kitchen, three small kitchens, and twenty-four smaller stage kitchens that only served patients. It also had five cafeterias. It served a total of approximately 10,000 meals per day. The challenge was intriguing but enormous. I didn't know if I was capable of handling the job, but I decided to go for an interview, as long as everything was kept confidential.

The Henry Ford Hospital was located in the New Center area of Detroit. The edifice alone was like a small town and very impressive. As I walked through the lobby to my interview, I was intimidated by the vast space and the number of people walking in every direction. After three progressive interviews, including the last with the CEO, and few sleepless nights, I received a call from human resources saying the job was mine and that I would get almost double the salary that I was presently making. I took the job, telling myself that this was the chance of a lifetime, that it would shape my career as a chef. During the interview process, I had been told that I would have a free hand in changing all the dishes, writing recipes, training cooks and kitchen staff, and restoring food quality for patients and hospital personnel. I took it very seriously.

The first day on the job, I was given a tour of the department by Director of Dietary, Peter Muoio, who introduced me to all the key hospital personnel, supervisors, managers, dietitians, and cooks. He remained my boss for a few years, until he took a job at another hospital. Everyone greeted me with a big welcome, delighted that the food quality was about to change. On the way to the main kitchen, where I would be directing all activities, Peter Muoio said, "Don't be discouraged by the immensity of the place. The food here is so bad that any dishes you change, especially in the cafeteria, will make you a hero. Take your time. Give yourself a few days to walk around and write notes before you implement any changes. I don't expect a miracle overnight." That tour lasted most of the morning.

I was left in my new office, reflecting on how long it would take to gain control of the Henry Ford Hospital kitchens and what my first steps should be. I decided to make my rounds and visit my cooks. It didn't take long before I had my first challenge, an encounter with one of the staff.

David said he had recently been promoted to the position of cook after washing pots and pans. As he opened large cans of Campbell's tomato soup, he informed me that we didn't have enough electric can openers and I should arrange to buy more. I said yes and walked away to the next station. Suddenly I was stopped by an unpleasant noise, so I turned around, only to see the method Dave was using to heat the cream of tomato soup. He was standing in front of a fifty-gallon pot, pouring tomato soup into the pot along with the metal lids of the cans! At first I thought it was a mistake, but after watching several lids fall into the pot, I felt compelled to intervene and ask the obvious question: Why the lids? Dave replied that perhaps I had never worked with those pots before. He pointed to the bottom of the pot, to a knob that opened and closed a one-inch spout where the soup would come out. He said that when the soup was hot, only the liquid would be released and the lids would remain in the pot. Stunned by the response, I calmly walked him over to the pots-and-pans area and told him that he would be a better pot-washer than a cook, my first decision of my new job!

Thus, I began to comprehend the skills of my cooks and the enormous challenge facing me. The cooks were all over fifty years old, many with health restrictions and many with over thirty years of service at the hospital. They moved very slowly. I knew I needed more talent and younger personnel. One by one, I found a way for those cooks to get early retirement with full benefits, which made them very happy. Vacating many positions allowed me to hire a sous-chef and talented cooks.

My father-in-law introduced me to talk radio, which I found to be very informative. One of my favorite talk show hosts of the time, Marc Scott, would begin his show by saying *Deus ex machina* (literally, "God from the machine"), a phrase originally used in Greek and Roman drama to indicate a god introduced into a play to resolve the entanglements of the plot. This phrase generally suggests any contrived solution to an insoluble difficulty. With this in mind, I proceeded with one cook at a time, one station at a time, one change at a time, and success began to show. I shared this success with my colleagues, food service workers, supervisors, managers, and all the dietitians, who helped me tremendously.

Learning different diets made me a better chef and more versatile in my career. Soon I gained confidence and the respect of every doctor, nurse, and administrator. For years the patients' food had had reputation as being tasteless. I worked hard to change that, suggesting the same menu items for patients and employees. I felt that if I could keep the nurses and doctors happy, they would become my sales people. How? Since they were eating in the cafeteria the same dishes that the patients were being served, they would know how good it tasted, and, in turn, they would encourage the patients to eat! I started a policy of personally visiting a patient with a dietitian each time a problem arose regarding the food. I would accommodate and cook whatever the patients desired (as long as it was in line with the doctor or dietician's prescription). If I didn't have it one day, I would provide it the next. Within a few years I had built a top-notch cooking staff.

Administrators from other hospitals came to visit my food service operation. Some would contract with me through the hospital, hiring me to implement the same ideas in their cafeterias and patient services. I consulted at Lakewood Hospital in Cleveland; Sisters of Mercy Hospital in Joliet, Illinois; St. Mary's Hospital in Madison, Wisconsin; St. Joseph Mercy Hospital in Ann Arbor and St. Joseph Mercy Oakland Hospital in Pontiac, Michigan.

I always applied the same principles that had worked in the past: hiring a capable chef, firing or training the existing one, menu changes, writing new recipes, and controlling food and labor costs. The name Chef Beato became well known both locally and nationally. I was obsessed with the new challenges, and I wanted more. I loved the recognition and the attention I was getting, and I became more and more motivated.

The director of food services, my boss, Gary Severn, asked me if I would meet with a part-time evening employee—a tray-passer for patients, who claimed that she was interested in becoming a chef. He felt she needed some guidance. The next day she came to work an hour early to meet me. Her name was Terry Brigs. Normally, a young girl meeting the executive chef would be shy and nervous. Terry entered my office with a big smile on her face and said, "I was wondering where all the good food came from as I passed dinner trays to the patients. I didn't know this hospital had a real chef or that this great kitchen existed!" This petite, extremely pleasant young girl said she worked at the hospital part-time while studying at Oakland Community College and was told by her teacher that she should find a certified food service with a chef who was willing and able to teach an apprentice on-site for three years. She said, "Seeing the food that I've been serving our patients, I didn't have to look anywhere else. I am determined to become a chef. Would you please help me?" She had the courage and the resolve to become a chef, and I had the talent to make it happen.

I became a member of the Michigan Chefs de Cuisine Association, to which all the best-known chefs belonged. Before long, I was serving on the board as a trustee, and later as vice president, as well as an advisor for the apprenticeship program at Oakland Community College. I took the executive chef course, recognized by the American Culinary Federation, and became a certified executive," CEC" I also convinced my boss at the hospital to implement an in-house apprenticeship program. Anyone who wanted to become a chef could go to college one day a week to learn the fundamentals of the culinary field. Then they would work forty hours a week under my direction for three years. It was a 6000-hour course during which they would be assigned to different culinary stations. They would log their hours and write one recipe per week, which I reviewed and endorsed, so that if and when they graduated, they would have their own cookbook.

The program was extremely rewarding for me because I had an opportunity to give back through teaching, and also because it provided the hospital the possibility of hiring fully trained cooks, tailor-trained to work in our operations. It was a win-win situation for the hospital, the cooks, and myself. The first two students to join the program were Terry Briggs and Ramon Herrera. Through their dedication and hard work, they not only made the program successful, but also brought out the teaching skills I didn't know I had and made me proud. After graduation, they went on to teach culinary arts at the college level. Moreover, they became Mr. and Mrs. Herrera, and today, they are still successful culinary teachers.

After that, whenever an opportunity arose to teach or to give a speech, I always used their stories as a symbol of success. Both had come from poor minority families, and both proved that by working hard with commitment, anyone could make it in this country.

During the nineteen years that I worked for the Henry Ford Hospital, I always tried to advance by creating new challenges for myself.

When I first joined the association, I met another member, Chef Mario Etemad, and we became friends. To this day, we love each other like brothers. We took the executive chef course at the same time, and soon afterwards, Mario took a job as executive chef at St. Joseph Hospital in Pontiac, Michigan.

I balanced work with family, attending my children's sporting events; Both Robert and Kelli were very athletic. So there were many soccer, basketball, volleyball and hockey games. The latter was the most nerve-wracking sport for me, because I was the goalie's father. Our family shared lots of love. As parents, Judy and I made sure that our children had everything. We worked hard, working all different shifts, keeping different hours in order to avoid the need for babysitters, and making sacrifices to meet our goals and commitment as parents. We were not rich, nor were we poor. Thankfully we had good health which God had provided to us, so that we could work hard and see our children through college and on to marriage.

Chef Milos Cihelka was the founder of the Michigan Chefs de Cuisine. In 1986, when the association had about 200 members, he and Chef Camille Kassem selected seven chefs to form a culinary team in Michigan that would compete in the 1988 Culinary Olympics in Frankfurt, Germany. Chef Milos would be the manager and Chef Camille would be the team captain. They would draft six of the most talented chefs—who, had already won a gold medal and were in good standing with the association as a professional chef (and met many other requirements). To join their team. Chef Milos and Chef Camille set the rules. Once they made the team, the chefs were to train for two years, enter different local and world competitions, win at least a silver medal in every competition, and participate in fund-raisers to pay for travel expenses. Any chef who didn't win a silver medal was disqualified, and another chef was chosen to replace him or her. The chefs would get permission from their employers to take time off from work to participate in any event required by the team leaders.

Chef Milos and Chef Camille were going to announce the final decisions at the next meeting, a month later.

The entire membership was happy, and many of us hoped to be picked. Having won gold, silver, and bronze medals in previous competitions made me a contender, but since the pool of talented chefs was large, I was both hopeful and skeptical. Being a member of this team and winning gold in Frankfurt went beyond my childhood dreams of coming to America. When the team members where announced, I was not one of them, but I cheered for those who were picked and made a commitment to support the team in any way possible to bring gold to Michigan.

During that time, Scott Cummings, one of the best cooks on my staff quit his position at Henry Ford Hospital to take a job as executive chef at Cottage Hospital in Grosse Pointe, Michigan. I gave him my blessing. He later became a member of the health care culinary team.

At Henry Ford, Jules Bouthilet was the top administrator of the Dietary, Laundry, and other departments. He reported to the hospital CEO. He took great interest in our department and often commented that it was the best of all his departments. He wanted a clear line to me, the executive chef of the hospital, without having to go through my boss, Gary Severn. He was an admirer of great food. Whenever he booked a lunch with other administrators or doctors, I made sure it was superb. Jules often came directly to the kitchen afterwards to congratulate me and my staff for a job well done, and he often told my boss, the Director of Dietary, that I was the backbone of the department. Once a year, our management staff got a pay raise, and he always made sure I got what I deserved.

When we had tryouts for new dishes, I always invited Jules to taste the food. When we opened a coffee shop in the front lobby, he took a great interest in the menu items. Gary Severn told me that he loved my relationship with Jules, and that it made his job much easier. The opening of the coffee shop was a great success. Both employees and visitors gave great comments. It was another job well done, according to Jules.

Two months after the opening of the coffee shop, my boss received a phone call from Jules's boss, the hospital CEO, Doug Peters (who reported to the president and hospital board members). Doug Peters wanted to know why we didn't serve Vlasic Dill Pickles in the coffee shop, since Mr. Vlasic was a board member. He told him that he would speak to me. By the time I got the message, all hell had broken loose. My simple explanation was that when I was doing research for a fresh three-day pickle, Vlasic didn't make it, so I had chosen the best I could find in that category. Jules was upset that his boss, the CEO, was demanding that explanation. He asked my opinion regarding which pickle was best to serve with the sandwiches I created, and my response was simple:

our present one. Jules said the case was closed and that he would deal with my boss. A few months later we switched to Vlasic pickles. Jules was a man of integrity, but he lost to the powers above him.

When Jules resigned to take a position as the CEO of Lakewood Hospital in Cleveland, the first project on his agenda was to improve the food service and bring it up to the standard maintained at Henry Ford. His main complaint was that the executive chef didn't know what he was doing. He did not stand out among his staff the way Chef Beato did at Henry Ford. He wore a hair net, not a chef's hat, so he looked like a barber, and his food had no flair. Jules pleaded with our administration to allow me to visit to asses the Lakewood Hospital kitchen and make recommendations.

Bernie Starkey took Gary Severn's job and became director of Dietary. He was the best boss I could ever ask for. He always encouraged me, and had faith in me and a strong belief that I could do the job.

Lakewood Hospital in Cleveland became my first consulting job. When I was introduced to Jim Perko, executive chef, he knew the reason for my visit. When I asked him what the problem was, he bluntly told me to advise a replacement for him, because the new administrator didn't like him. I relayed that I was only there to observe and make recommendations.

During my three-day visit assessing the whole department, I spent lot of time with Jim. I came to the conclusion that Jim had talent and was a good chef. The problem was that he didn't know how to handle his position, dealing with the administration. Before I returned to

Detroit, I assured Jim that I liked him and said the problem could be easily solved. He replied, "So I'm not fired?" I left him with a promise that I would talk to the administrator and write a report suggesting keeping him on as a chef. My decision did not sit well with the administrator. I had a hard time convincing him that Jim should retain his position. Two weeks later, my boss sent me back to Cleveland to work with Jim for as long as it would take to change his image in the eyes of the administrators into one that compared with Chef Beato's.

The first thing I did was make sure he looked like a chef: dressed in a chef's toque and starched white coat. For six months, I spent two or three days a week in Cleveland. I changed the patients' menu, introduced new dishes in the cafeteria, and created a special menu for the doctors' dining room. Little by little, Jules started to appreciate Chef Jim's progress.

In October of that year, the American Culinary Federation (ACF) held a competition in Cleveland, and the Michigan chapter was expected to compete. This represented a great chance for Jim and his staff to represent the hospital—and what a great way to show the administration and convince them of his talent! When I proposed the idea to Jim, he loved it, but agreed to enter only as long as I stayed to help and direct all activities, because he had confidence in my leadership.

The first thing I had to do was convince my boss, Bernie Starkey, that it was okay to suggest my plan to the hospital administration. He replied that it was all right as long as I felt it would bring recognition to Henry Ford and a winning medal to Lakewood Hospital in Cleveland. It was a risk, but one that Jim and I were willing to take. The administration approved the project with much excitement.

The night before the competition, many hospital workers came by the Lakewood Hospital kitchen to wish us good luck, including Jules. The following day, when the judges' decision was announced, Jim won gold, as well as "Best of the Show," with a medal that excelled above all the gold medals. Jim and the hospital CEO became best friends, and Jim went on to be a competitor on the east regional USA culinary team. Jules traveled to Germany to watch Jim win gold at the Culinary Olympics in 1992. The Michigan Culinary Team also competed and won gold. They were very impressed that the Cleveland Lakewood Hospital had won gold, but they never knew that I'd had any involvement with them.

Because of the energy generated by the Michigan culinary team in the ACF, and inspired by having lead a hospital to win the gold medal in Cleveland for the first time, I got fired up and came up with the idea of creating my own team. I would call it the Health Care Culinary Team. First I convinced my best friend, Chef Mario Etemad, a key member of our future success, to form the team with me. Together, we convinced four additional chefs from other Detroit hospitals, as well as Chef Jim from Cleveland, to join our team and enter the local competition that was scheduled to take place six months later at Detroit's Cobo Hall. Chef Mario and I surmised that the reason we hadn't been picked for the Michigan Chefs de Cuisine team might have been that we were hospital chefs, rather than fancy restaurant or hotel chefs. We felt that we had something to prove. Hospitals chefs could have talent equal to that of chefs everywhere.

After six months of trial runs, hard work, and dedication, with the slight logistical complication that one of our chefs lived in Cleveland, we managed to coordinate all our ideas and get ready for the big event. Two weeks before the day, we discovered that the Michigan Culinary team was competing, too. We felt that the pressure was on them and we had nothing to lose, because we were a Cinderella team. We competed in the same category that they did. We were a five-man team for the Grand Buffet plus two more members of their team competed in the individual category. With the permission of Ford Hospital, the team used our kitchen to do the final preparation. We worked all night to the tunes of Billy Joel's famous song, "Pressure"

At 6:00 a.m. we loaded all the food into a hospital van and made two trips to Cobo Hall. It was a cold March morning with light snow on the streets. Our truck drove very slowly, with team members holding trays and racks full of food, ready to be assembled at the hall before the judges entered at 8:30. By some miracle we got everything done in time.

Then we packed up all our empty pans, extra platters, and racks of leftover food, and headed back to the hospital, all of us freezing because we were only wearing our chef jackets. I was driving slowly in the right lane on the Lodge Freeway while the rest of the team, exhausted from lack of sleep The others were lying down all over the van. The traffic was light since it was a Sunday morning.

Suddenly, my left front tire shot out of the shaft, flew ahead of the van, and crossed the cement median like a bullet. It rolled into the oncoming lanes and hit the side fender of a car traveling south before it stopped moving on the side of the road. I managed to guide the van to the ditch, as pots and pans flew all over the team members. Everybody was shaken up. Without any phones to call for help, I crossed the freeway with a team member, jumped over a fence, and walked to look for a place where we could use the phone. Four blocks on we came to a motel and called Ford Hospital Security to come and rescue us. By the time we'd made our way back to the van, the Detroit Police were there, as well the hospital security guards. We were relieved that no one was hurt, and the security guards drove us back to our cars at the hospital. I went home to rest until 6:00 p.m., when I would have to return to Cobo Hall to be in time for the awards ceremony.

Our Health Care team won gold! The Michigan Chefs team won gold, and their two individual chefs won silver and bronze. We lost the Grand Prize by just two percentage points. We were on cloud nine and were the talk of the show. Other chefs were wondering where we had come from. We proved to the entire Michigan Chefs de Cuisine Association that the Heath Care Culinary Team was second to none.

After having been up all night, I went home to sleep. At 6:00 p.m. the team reunited with fresh minds to celebrate our gold medal. We agreed that had we lost the wheel on the way to the competition, with the van full of food, it simply would have destroyed us. After a delicious meal with good wine, we discussed how we would move the team forward and questioned what it would take to go to the Olympics. We had proved that we had talent, but we where flat broke, while the Michigan team had already raised $40,000. Our task seemed enormous and unreachable. None of us worked in fancy restaurants or hotel facilities that would be able to come up with the funds. Nevertheless, because we were so pumped up, we decide "never to say never", to stay in touch, and to explore the future. We ended the celebrations early, deciding to meet again in a month.

When I got home at 9:00, there was a message from Chef Milos, the head of the Michigan team, saying to call him. After he congratulated me and said how proud he was of me, for leading the team to win the gold medal. He offered me a spot on the Michigan team. Stunned and confused by the offer, I told him that I would give him an answer in two days, because I had to discuss it with the rest of my team. As tired as I was, I had a sleepless night. The realization set in that I might never get another chance at the Olympics, and that without funds, our Health Care team had a nearly impossible task. Nevertheless, I did not want to jump ship without sharing the news with my team members. When I did, all the chefs on my team supported the idea and strongly encouraged me to join the Michigan team, and go and kick ass in Germany, and maybe in four years lead them there. Without hesitation, I called Chef Milos to accept his offer, only to find out that they had let one of their team members go and I would be filling his position. But there was a stipulation: I would have to participate in another competition in Chicago in two months and win a gold medal in order to be accepted on the team. He said that would make sure I was for real.

At that point I was not about to let any obstacle interfere with my ultimate goal, so once again, up against a challenge, I accepted. In Chicago, I won gold again and was welcomed into the folds of the Michigan team. We had a very busy schedule of tryouts, fund-raising events, and an international competition thirty days later in Vancouver, Canada. Feeling like the underdog again, I had lot of catching up to do in preparation for the big event.

A week before the event, we got the news that my grandma had died in New York. Some of my family, including my mom and dad, attended the funeral. I missed it because of my work and team schedule. It was a sad day for me, and even more so for my dad, who had known his mom for just a few short years. I was lucky that I had my family's full support and much understanding from my wife, who carried on with all the functions of the family

My schedule at work was very demanding, but I was blessed to have the full support of my boss, the administrators, and the 400 dietary employees, who all cheered for me.

The Michigan team, which had seven members, decided to compete outside the US as a trial run, to experience all the difficulties of traveling and to learn to overcome any situations we might encounter when we went to the Olympics in Germany. Competing in our first international competition was very hard and stressful. We had to pack the food in appropriate containers with particular specifications. They had to fit in the overhead compartments in the airplane and maintain the right temperature to minimize spoilage. We brought all the tools we would need, including a selection of knives. Our *modus operandi* was to check our clothes but keep our food and tools with us. Can you imagine traveling today with all the knives in your hand luggage in a plane? We declared everything with a brief explanation of all the ingredients used in the well-prepared and wrapped food, and convinced Canada customs to let us into Canada. The most convincing argument for customs was that the food was not for consumption, but only for display in a competition, and then it would be discarded.

One of the members of the MCCA worked as a chef for Northwest Airlines. He pulled some strings to give us a corner of their Vancouver kitchen to use for the final stage in the competition, over the next five days. Packing was the most important thing—we couldn't forget any essential ingredients.

I was well aware that this first international competition and my first time competing with this new team would shine the light on my status as a chef. The day before I was to compete, I was missing my old team members and feeling a little out of place with the new ones, I was coming back from a short trip to the produce market with four chefs on my team. As I exited the back of the van, someone accidently closed the sliding door on my left hand. It was painfully bruised but not broken, so I could manage at the competition. Thank God it wasn't my right hand.

I entered into two categories, both in garde manger. (cold food display), which included a meat platter, a seafood platter, and a platter of hors d'oeuvres, each with eight items for a total of sixty-four. The other was a lunch for four displayed cold, including soup, an appetizer, an entrée of your choice, salad, and dessert. I was awarded a gold medal for my platters and a bronze for the luncheon for 4. These results pointed out the areas that I needed to improve on. The rest of my team was awarded gold in the grand buffet. I was happy with the outcome but felt that I was the weak link.

Back home, after a few fund-raisers including a lunch for Governor James Blanchard at Michigan State University, the team earned $20,000. That put us in a very good financial position. Therefore, we decided that we could afford to each take an apprentice to Germany, provided that he was presently enrolled in the apprenticeship program. He or she had to be in good standing, and had to be already entered in the upcoming local competition, and won gold in the apprentice category. It was also decided that we needed another international competition under our belt, one that was held out of the country, before the granddaddy of them all, Germany. Singapore was coming up in few months. It was said to be as tough as Germany, not only because of the talent that we had to face, but also because of the traveling.

The task seemed to be getting more and more complicated, balancing all the activities. First, I had to prep my apprentice, Ramon Herrera, for the local competition so he would win gold. Chef Milos was cracking the whip, demanding that the team have a practice run every three weeks so that he and the other master chefs could judge our work and give us constructive criticism. After tearing our work apart and demanding that we do better in the next practice, the judges told us that if we thought they were tough, they would be easy in comparison to the judges waiting for us in Singapore!

To be honest, I never thought I could satisfy Chef Milos in any practice run, and after some time I felt demoralized to the point of wanting to quit. But that word did not exist in my vocabulary because I had a goal and a dream to get to the Olympics. My apprentice Ramon won the gold medal that earned him a spot as an apprentice on the team. The importance of having my own apprentice with me was huge. During the practice run, Ramon could read my mind in every move that I made. He seemed always to be one step ahead, and that made my task much easier.

The first time I met Ramon was at a career day event at a Detroit high school. I was invited to participate with others chefs to hold interviews with the students so they could acquire information to find a job. Among the many students I talked to, Ramon had a certain demeanor that made him soar above the others. Even the teachers believed so. I was approached by one teacher who insisted that I be the chef to interview Ramon, because he was a good student who needed good guidance. After talking to many others, I finally got to him. He was a very impressive young man—well dressed, polite, and sure of what he wanted to be. After a long interview, I told him to look me up after college if he still wanted to be a chef. I didn't hear from him until three years later, when he called to share the good news that he had finished college and it was time for him to pursue a career in the culinary arts. I kept my promise and hired him as an apprentice.

Preparing for Singapore was a lot tougher than preparing for Vancouver because of the distance. We had to make sure the food stayed safe for the nineteen-hour flight. We arrived in the spring of 1988, in very hot weather. We stayed in a large hotel, and because of the competition, they gave us full run of their kitchen from midnight to 6:00 a.m. to prepare for our final presentation. We went shopping for food items during the day, got a little sleep in the evening, and worked through the night. The kitchen was big, but there was no air conditioning. With the windows open, it was over ninety degrees. Working with gelatin in such warm conditions was difficult—this was the sort of obstacle that we didn't expect while planning in Michigan, and only one of the obstacles we had to overcome.

The night before my competition, I consolidated the hotel food from two small walk-in refrigerators to one and executed my work from inside the other, which was twice the size of a phone booth. We hired a company with two refrigerator vans and no windows. I guessed that they belonged to a meat market. There was just enough room to fit all my platters, but I insisted on not riding in front with the driver, so I sat in the back on the floor, squeezing my body between the platters and holding one on my lap. The competition hall was twenty minutes away. I asked the driver to go very slowly because we had plenty of time. The communication was done with gestures because he didn't speak English. When he closed the back door, a dim light went on so I was not in darkness. I sat there, watching my work bounce with every bump he drove over, worrying that any of my delicate pieces might break. I glanced at the upper corner of the van, saw a steel bar running from one side of the truck to the other, and thought it must be used to hang meat. In the far corner, hanging from the steel bar, was a plastic bag containing some kind of dark liquid. It dangled over one of my platters. All I could do was pray that the bag would not bust or leak over my platter. The ride was stressful and it felt like a two-hour drive instead of twenty minutes. Wearing only a chef jacket, I was cold and half frozen when we arrived at the hall, but I was happy and relieved that the plastic bag hadn't broken.

I went on to set my food on the table and was ready for the judges with forty minutes to spare. All I wanted was to rest in my bed at the hotel room, but I had to stay and guard my table until the judges entered the hall. We had been told by the advisory team not to leave our table unattended, in case any jealous competitor passed by and sabotaged our work by moving or stealing a couple of pieces.

When I got to the hotel, I met some of my team members, who invited me to join them for breakfast, but I was too tired and stressed to eat. All I wanted to do was lie down and rest. With a terrible headache, I lay down. Chills came over me, so I took a Tylenol, covered myself with all the blankets I could find, closed my eyes, and fell asleep.

I woke up to the ringing telephone. Confused, I answered. One of my team member said that the van was leaving in thirty minutes for the awards ceremony. I got up, opened the curtains, went to the bathroom, turned on the light, and looked in the mirror. I was covered with brown spots—all over my chest and my back. I thought it was my own feces, but it had no odor. I went back to the bed, only to find two silver dollar-size chocolates wrapped in gold foil, left by the cleaning staff the day before. It had melted all over the sheets. Relieved that it was just chocolate, I took a quick shower and got to the van in time.

We all scored gold medals! Finally, for the first time, I saw Chef Milos smile. He told us how proud he was to be our team manager, and then casually warned us of the big challenge that faced us in Germany in October. He warned us that none of this would count if we didn't get a medal in Germany, whatever the color—bronze, silver, or gold.

With only few months to prepare, we increased to two practice runs a month. By the time I reached Germany, I could prepare my dishes with my eyes closed, and still, all we heard at the practice runs from Chef Milos was how unprepared we were and that we all underestimated what it would take to win a medal at the Frankfurt Olympics. As October approached, we all decided to enter the "individuals" contests. We could pick which day of the week we wanted to participate, from Monday to Friday, with the option to compete on two days in order to get a better shot at the gold. I stated that I wanted to compete on Wednesday and only once, because if I missed the gold or any medal with my best dishes on the first run, certainly my secondary dishes would not achieve any better results.

Three team members decided to enter twice. Because we were well financed, we each had three sets of clothing: travel clothes, a white chef coat and toque to wear in the team parade, as well as a suit for team pictures and the awards presentation. We dressed alike with the Michigan culinary logo. I was very proud to be part of it all.

During our nine-hour flight to Germany, I tried to relax and sleep, but due to excitement and stress, I was awake the whole time. I reflected on where I was, the mission at hand, and how far I had come. I thought of the fourteen-year-old boy I had been, trying to break the hold of poverty and realize my dream of reaching America, with no clear vision or method, escaping from all that had held my family back. I had never been a very religious person, but I believed in God, and to quote one of my favorite talk show hosts, the famous Rush Limbaugh, "with talent on loan from God," I knew I would do well. I had taken two weeks' vacation from work, the first for Germany and the second to visit my dad in Italy, where he was spending the summer and fall.

The accommodations in Germany were good. The kitchen was provided by Nestlé in a house that was quite far from the hotel and from the Olympics hall. The first day of the competition, two of our team members won gold. The second day, another won gold. That really put pressure on me and another team member, who were competing on Wednesday.

Three certified Master Chefs (the highest level of chef possible) accompanied us as staff members and advisors: Master Chef Milos (the manager), Master Pastry Chef Leon, and Master Chef Leopold. Among many other important things, they checked the hall before we arrived to make sure it was set up properly, with fresh linens and well-arranged center pieces.

In the morning, around 4:00 am, Chef Milos was to arrive with Chef Leopold to help us assemble the platters. Ramon and I were in the cafeteria having breakfast when Chef Milos walked in ranting and raving and questioning us for being on a break when our work was not complete. I replied that all our work was done and we were only waiting for him to assemble the platters. Later, he apologized.

My other team member was having difficulty and was behind schedule, so the rest of the team stepped in to help. The reason that only Chef Milos was allowed to assemble the platters was that he had slept all night, so he was relaxed, and with a fresh mind. This step would minimize the risk of mistakes. All platters had to be assembled for eight persons, each having identical garnishes. At 6:00 in the morning, when you were tired and under stress, it was easy to miscount. That is where team work comes in!

My dishes consisted of a meat platter, a seafood platter, and eight different hors d'oeuvres. Many competitors decorated their tables with expensive props and flowers. I decided to make six long-stem roses out of pasta dough to decorate my table in a very simple and elegant way. Our team manger's philosophy was that there was no talent in buying flowers, and the judges couldn't care less how much the decorations cost because they concentrated only on the food. Their emphasis was on whether it was clean, nutritionally balanced, innovative, well presented, affordable, and practical.

That Wednesday morning, when Chef Milos finished assembling my platters, he told Chef Camille, the team captain, in a low voice that we should "kick ass" with these platters. He didn't know I heard him. For the rest of the day, until the awards ceremony at 6:00 p.m., I kept hearing those words in my mind. I thought, "What if he is wrong? Am I a contender for a medal? If not, I will be disappointed, but content because just being there is a great achievement." At the awards ceremony I was sitting in the first row with Chef Milos, Ramon, and some staff members. The rest of the team was preparing for tomorrow's event. The hall was packed with chefs and supporters from around the world.

The awards would be either a medal or a diploma. A medal was great achievement but a diploma was a gesture of thanks to the participant. They always started to call bronze medals, then sliver, then gold, and then the diplomas. As many chefs where called and invited to the podium to receive their medals, with every category that passed, I became more nervous. Sweat was dripping down my face. We finally got to the gold category, and my name was not called. I sat with anticipation, hoping my name would be next. It was impossible that none of us had heard my name. Then they went on to the diploma category. My other team member, who had been in trouble early in the morning, managed to get gold. With faces overcome by fatigue and stress, my whole support team looked the same. Earlier, before we entered the hall, I had jokingly told my apprentice that if they called my name for a diploma, he should get up and get it. Now that joke was becoming realty. My consolation was that I was not the only one receiving a diploma, because there were many of them. The diploma category finally ended, and my name remained uncalled. I knew then that someone had overlooked my name, and as the ceremony went on to the next phase, I shared this thought with Chef Milos. There might have been a mistake.

He told me to sit, relax, and be patient until the end. So I followed his advice, sitting there, confused and distraught. Then I heard my name being called. The MC announced that Chef Joe Beato was awarded a gold medal with distinction! That meant the judges had given me a perfect score. Milos and rest of my supporters jumped up and down like children, because I was the first member of the team to receive a perfect score. Two of our other team member won the same award later in the competition. Perhaps Milos knew all along about the extra category. He either wanted to see me sweat, or he didn't want to ruin the surprise. At mid-morning the next day, I called home and my wife informed me that my award had been announced on the radio.

Soon after, the CEO of Henry Ford Hospital called and congratulated me on behalf of the entire staff. By the end of the competition the team had accumulated thirteen gold medals and it was time to celebrate. After a big dinner, the apprentices and the support staff packed all our equipment and took it back to home. The rest of the team toured a few cities in Italy.

I separated from my team to visit my dad in my home town. While I was there, my dad proudly showed my gold medal to everybody. It was ironic that my home town saw the gold medal first, before the rest of my family and the

US state of Michigan that I represented. Three days later I rejoined the team in Rome and we celebrated until it was time to depart for home.

I continued to work for the hospital for two more years, as I had a promise to keep. One year after Germany, with the backing of the Michigan Chefs de Cuisine Association, Chef Mario and I put together a new Michigan culinary team, implementing the same process that had been used for the previous team. My longtime friend-brother Mario became captain, while I managed all the financial aspects, including travel and accommodations, team appearances, fund raising, the dress code, and securing a good location where we could work in Germany. For skills development, we drafted a long-time friend, and perhaps one of the best chefs in the world, Team USA gold medal winner Dan Hugelier, He proceeded to coach our team to another solid gold victory in the 1992 Olympics. That year, we won a total of five gold medals.

My competitions where over, as I was burned out from stress. Yet I was always looking for a new challenge. I continued to work hard for the Michigan Chefs Association, and twice won the Chef of the Year award. After a while, I felt that I needed new projects. I realized I was addicted to stress and took a part-time teaching job at Wayne County Community College, The college hired me to teach and prepare ten students for a local competition that would be held in four months. The college had never done well, with the excuse of being in an urban area with a minority student body. I took up the challenge of making believers of my students. I wanted them to win, and any reason why they couldn't would be a cheap excuse. With some of them it was a real challenge.

One of my female student's mother attended a class to check on me because her daughter felt singled out and picked on. I had no problem with that, because I remembered feeling the same way when I was first challenged on the Michigan team. I applied the same principle for the girl (and her mom) that I had applied on myself, either learn and be rewarded or quit. The mother never came back. She knew I was doing the right thing by her daughter. Every one of my students got a medal in the competition. The total score was five gold, four silver, and one bronze. The bronze was awarded to the girl who had felt picked on. Both mother and daughter apologized to me and thanked me for being tough and making a believer out of her.

The Wayne County Community College administrators where very happy with the results. For the first time, their students and the college were recognized in the culinary field. Two months later, they contacted me again. They said that their two gold medal winners were raising funds to compete in Las Vegas and wondered if I train them, and travel to the competition, because they had confidence in me.

Judy and I decided to make a small vacation out of it. Peter Sugamelli, one of their regular teachers and a fine chef, would travel and share responsibilities with me all the way to the end. Our two competitors entered in the college category. The morning of the competition, after the four of us had worked all night and they had set up their table, Peter and I suggested that the students go to bed and rest, as they had to appear in full uniform at the awards ceremony at 6:00 p.m. The hall doors closed after the judges walked in. Peter and I decided to try our luck at the slots machines. After losing a few dollars each, we heard our names announced over the intercom, asking us to appear at the hall a.s.a.p. We looked at each other with a blank look and made our way to the hall. There, three judges greeted us. They shared with us that they had never seen such sophisticated, upscale college work, and we had two choices. One was to leave our students' display in the college category, in which case it would not be judged, and would not win any award; the second was to change the status and enter at the professional level. We chose the latter.

At six o'clock, we met the students and informed them of the situation, and our decision … They were worried that they would not win a medal, and we shared their concerns, but there was nothing anybody could do. I felt that it was partly my fault as I had taught them such advanced dishes and techniques. Perhaps I should have toned it down, but wanting the best for the students and the college, I had put forth my best effort. This effort re-sulted in two students being awarded gold medals, and a trophy for best display.

Still looking for challenge, I decided to give back to society. I worked hard to help implement the MCCA's participation in the ACF (American Chefs Federation) program, "Chefs Against Hunger." I worked for a few years raising money for Easter Seals to help children with scoliosis, and for a few years with March of Dimes to help children with birth defects. Meanwhile, I saw an opportunity to buy a restaurant located two blocks from Henry Ford Hospital. It was a decision based on very mixed emotions to leave the hospital, realizing all the benefits security, and opportunities it had provided to me for so many years. But my children had grown up. Judy was still working as a nurse. And it was time to move on to my next challenge.

As a chef, I'd had very little experience in the restaurant business. I'd often argued with my colleagues about the degree of difficulty for a chef in a fancy restaurant versus a hospital. I always trumped, saying if a couple entered a restaurant with soft music playing and a beautiful ambiance, as they sipped a glass of wine, waiting for their favorite dish to arrive, how much talent was needed to make them happy? Compare that to preparing a meal for a very sick person who has a poor appetite is frustrated by the hospital staff making his or her bed, or is angry with the nurses who are too busy to attend his needs. He is upset with his doctor who is late. His lunch or dinner tray is the only thing that might make his day, and then add in his dietary restrictions. The food had better be appealing and tasty. That was my challenge as a hospital chef.

I opened my first restaurant, Il Centro, specializing in Italian cuisine. It was located in the New Center Area of Detroit. I quickly learned that it took a lot more than just being a good chef to be successful. There were many other elements involved. There were the complicated finances, the politics of getting a liquor license, meetings with attorneys to draft legal papers, as well as architects and interior decorators. Then there were the food critics who stormed in on opening day, while the staff was still learning to pronounce the names of the dishes on the menu and were most likely to make mistakes. It was an enormous experience. Having my name at the top of the culinary world as a gold medal chef only meant that the food critics had higher expectations, and would take more shots at me, whether justifiably or not.

I took my punishment and worked to make things better. The restaurant was located just a block from Henry Ford Hospital. As a result many of my customers were hospital staff, doctors, nurses, and administrators who missed my food at the hospital. Also I was located across from the Fisher Theater, a very well established theater for Broadway plays that came into town. I had a very successful nine years. During that time my nephew, Joe Beato, son of my younger brother, Vito, became my apprentice. Being able to teach a member of my family was extra special for me, particularly because it would continue the legacy with our common name. Joe did very well in his third year of the MCCA apprenticeship program at Oakland Community College. He entered a culinary competition, as all third-year students are required to do, and won an ACF gold medal.

Running a restaurant may be the most stressful and toughest job there is. With long hours, I was burning the candle at both ends. My body became weak, I experienced severe headaches, and in the 1999 I was diagnosed with Hepatitis C. This illness was rare at Ford Hospital. The doctors told me there was little they could do, and prescribed a medication that had a forty percent cure rate. I was told to rest and not to work so hard. I had lots of time to think about whether or not to take the drug. After a while, I was forced to sell the restaurant and put my working life on hold, as I became well acquainted with hepatitis C.

The doctors did a liver biopsy, and when they discovered where I was born, they traced the cause to my childhood. Growing up in my small town, whenever anyone got sick, the town doctor would prescribe an injection, and a lady who my mom knew administered it. I remember the syringe being very long, and once assembled, it was the scariest thing for a kid. Sanitary measures left much to be desired. The same syringe was used for everyone throughout the town. As a result, many people were infected with the virus.

I waited a year until a new, more potent drug with a ninety-percent chance of cure became available. I immediately started to take it. It would take one year to work, and I would have to endure the many side effects that came along with it. It was devastating, and I almost quit the process However, I did endure it to the end, with a lot of support and encouragement from my family. After a year of the medication, a blood test revealed that the virus was gone. Four years later, my older brother, John, came down with the same illness and struggled through the same treatment.

While my life was on hold for the time being, my nephew, Joe, got a temporary job in Rome, Italy. He spent nine months acquiring new skills and talents to bring home.

Four years later, my health rebounded, and" Make-a-Buck-Beato" (that's what my colleagues called me) was in business again. I teamed up with my younger brother, Vito, and opened an upscale restaurant called Via Nove on Nine Mile Road in Ferndale, Michigan. (*Via Nove* is Italian for Nine Mile, which explains how we came up with the name.) My nephew, Joe, became my chef, and he managed the bulk of the operation while I worked at his side. The venue had an area of about 10,000 square feet. We did all the receiving and cooking in the basement. The dining space was on three floors. There was a large bar located squarely in the center of the second floor dining room, with twenty-foot towering glass shelves that rose to the ceiling, full of every variety of liquor. We enjoyed great success and were very busy for the first four years. The restaurant was always packed on weekends, and reservations were required, sometimes two weeks in advance.

Work was hard and the hours were long, but with the family's help, things ran smoothly. The income was great. The bills and debts accumulated before opening were getting paid. Life was good and I was happy, but my body ached.

I had heard and read about conditions during the Great Depression, but I always assumed it would never happen again, because we now had all the knowledge and tools needed to prevent it. In 2008 one of the greatest recession occurred. The housing market was destroyed, the bank industry was in deep trouble, and politicians pointed fingers at each other while the work force collapsed and millions of people lost their jobs. Eating out in restaurants became considered a luxury. Unfortunately, eating out is one of the first things that families cut back on, especially high end restaurants like ours. For two years we'd had warning signs, but we never could have imagined the magnitude of what was coming.

We scaled back our work force. The family picked up the load, and we barely made ends meet. Fatigued and stressed from the pressures of business, we knew that drastic changes were imminent. A long-time friend from my Henry Ford Hospital days, Paul Hysen, hired me for consultation jobs at New York Presbyterian in Manhattan, and Stoney Brook Hospital in Long Island. I will always appreciate the timing of these jobs. The income from both kept me financially above water during a bad time.

Closing down was never an option, we confined the dining area to the ground floor, and because we had one of the most beautiful bars, we turned the second and third floors into a nightclub. Vito and his son-in-law, Mike, played a big part in hiring different disk jockeys, as well as managing the bar.

On Fridays and Saturdays, after 11:00 p.m., we went from having an empty restaurant to a packed house with 400 plus customers until 2:00 a.m. Business was good, and the income helped pay the bills. But managing a large intoxicated crowed was very difficult. Many nights when I stayed at work, I observed customers consuming a $12 or $14 drink within minutes and reordering another, and another, regardless of the cost. This compared to dinnertime, when I worked so hard to create an appetizer for $8, only to have a table of four or six people order one portion to share, because of the economy. Where was the logic? Two hours' income from the nightclub was greater than that of a full night's dining in the restaurant. It was hard for me to adapt to that life, but it was necessary.

In 2011 it was time for me to retire. My body demanded it. So we sold the business.

I am glad that I broke the hold and came to America, the land of the free, with opportunities for people to become whoever they want to be and to achieve whatever they desire through hard work, without any help or interference from the government. No matter what country I have lived in, my motto was love and respect for country but fear of the government.

Judy and I now enjoy retirement, splitting our time between Florida in the winter and our northern Michigan lake house in the summer. I continue to cook for my family and friends.

The best of my story would not be complete if I did not say that I have been blessed with the most beautiful gifts in life, three granddaughters who I love more than life itself. This book is dedicated to them, Gabriella, Samantha, and Gianna so that they may know and keep my legacy. And that they always remember that any dream is possible with hard work, perseverance, and dedication.

With my parents, Antony and Domenica Beato
Detroit, 1990

The Puglia Region of Southern Italy and the Truth about Olive Oil

The land was very fertile, and most of the people lived from it in many ways. Every season brought an abundance of fresh fruit and vegetables … In the spring, there were cherries, along with *fioroni*, a kind of large, juicy fig, plums, apricots, peaches, *nespole* (loquats), fava beans, and asparagus. Summer was the time for pears, prickly pears, almonds, the first grapes for eating (rather than wine), figs, and, of course, a superabundance of tomatoes. In the fall, we harvested grapes to make wine, olives, and grains to make flour. Our land produced so much produce that it was transported to other regions of Italy and throughout Europe. The biggest industry was olives and olive oil. As a chef, I would like to tell you how olive oil was made, the different categories, and how it is used best.

When we shop for olive oil, all the different labels tend to be very confusing. Starting with the high end, there is extra virgin olive oil, virgin olive oil, pure olive oil, blended olive oil, and pomace olive oil. Than comes the country where the olives are grown, and which is best: Greece, Italy, Spain, Portugal, California, USA, and so on. Only fifteen to twenty years ago, if we wanted olive oil in North America, we had to buy it from an imported foods stores, often one that stocked foods from a particular country. Only immigrants knew the differences between them.

Many Italian immigrants packed olive oil sealed in zinc cans in their luggage, when traveling to the U.S. or Canada. I brought two cans for my uncle in 1964. Back home in Italy, it was customary to ask people who were about to immigrate to America to do them the favor of transporting a couple of cans of oil for their relatives. At that time, everybody crossed the Atlantic by ship and there were no weight restrictions, while sending anything by air was far too costly. Over the years, as more and more immigrants crossed the ocean, America woke up and discovered pure olive oil's liquid gold taste, nutritional value, and diversity in cooking, as well as its profit potential.

Many people were ignorant about the differences indicated on various labels, the range of prices, and the culinary uses. Comedians even told jokes about extra virgin olive oil coming from ugly olives.

Today many cookbooks have been written and the public is much better informed now. However, misinformation is still propagated. Some stories I read said darker green olive oil was better than golden; or that pouring oil in a shallow bowl to see how fast it spread showed the measure of its density, as did dipping hard-crust bread into it and tasting. Some said the most creative labeling and packaging would make the oil sell for a higher price.

But all this misleading information was an outrage. The fancy packaging does not mean the product inside is any better. Sometimes, there was some truth to what was being said, but too often the marketers found ways of fooling the public, which bordered on cheating them. If, for example, the darker green color was more appealing, what would stop them from mixing in a few extra olive leaves at the grinding stage to add natural color? Moreover, olives grown in the mountainous Abruzzi region are naturally greener than olives produced in Liguria, closer to the ocean. By the sea, there is more sun, which makes the oil lighter in color but also lower in acidity. Don't be fooled by the color of the oil!

Here are some tips to help you choose the appropriate oil for particular dishes. This information could even save you money.

❀ If you fry meats or seafood, make a casserole, or prepare a vegetarian dish, and you desire a hint of the flavor of olive oil, use pomace oil, because it usually contains one or two per cent olive oil. The olive taste is not that important, and even if you choose the best oil, the results can be mediocre.

❀ If you cook pasta, sauté meats or seafood without sauce (just garlic or basil), use pure olive oil so that you don't lose the flavor of the olives.

❀ If you make a salad with various varieties of greens, or tomatoes, prepare cold seafood, fresh mozzarella, bruschetta, or even want to drizzle some on your pasta, use extra virgin olive oil (the most expensive grade), and you will taste the nutty flavor of the fresh olives as well as the outstanding aroma.

❀ When you buy olive oil, try a small quantity. Pour a little in a bowl, dip in a piece of bread, and taste It should be pleasant, nutty, and fragrant. Avoid it, if it stings your throat, because that means it has a high level of acidity.

❀ Always store olive oil in a cool place, away from direct sunlight. If the oil coagulates in a cold place, don't worry. That's normal. Just bring the oil container close to the heat and it will return to its original color and form.

❀ If you pre preparing a complex salad, such as sea food or octopus, to be stored in the refrigerator, to be eaten later, add all the other ingredients except the olive oil so the dish doesn't become thick, greasy and unappealing; always drizzle olive oil at the last minute.

As a chef, I conducted several blind tastings of different extra virgin olive oils, including both imported and local varieties from over twenty different companies and origins. Kirkland olive oil from Costco came out in the top three, even when compared with the most expensive oils. It is made locally from olives grown and imported from Italy. It's the best value for your dollar.

Just few more notes:

❀ Extra virgin refers to oil extracted from olives in the first cold press.

❀ Virgin refers to oil extracted from the same olives in the second cold press.

❀ Pure olive oil, made 100 per cent from olives that may be imported from different parts of the world, is produced after the second cold press. Before the pulp is pressed, it is revived through an injection of steam and heat, and that is why it is not called cold pressed.

❀ Pomace oil is produced by taking the dry composite of olive pulp that remains after the third press, and adding other oils to revive it and release the olive flavor. This allows it to be sold more economically than the other three grades.

❀ Olive oil is one of the longest known oils. It was used in ancient cultures, and for some it was sacred. The Egyptians anointed their dead with it for preservation. During the time of the Roman Empire, sages and poets wore crowns of olive branches that represented intellectual excellence. Roman rulers exempted many inhabitants of the empire from going to war if they were committed to farming olive trees and gave them half the product. When Noah received the pigeon, it had in its beak an olive branch, representing peace and forgiveness. Palm Sunday is celebrated with olive branches. Jesus was seized by soldiers in a garden of olive trees before the Crucifixion, and he died on a Cross made of olive wood. The ancients rubbed warm olive oil on the body to soothe pain. Olive trees can survive for over 3000 years.

I suggest that you do your homework. Don't think that the olive oil that is most expensive should be the best. Buy to your taste, because to search for the purest and most sacred would be to take your own olives to the Trappeto oil presses and watch your own oil being made. I witnessed this process many times in my youth when I was earning money by picking olives.

Recipes from the Puglia Region of Southern Italy

Pane e Pomodoro—Tomatoes Bruschetta
4 servings

1 cup fresh vine-ripened tomatoes, diced
2 cloves garlic, chopped fine
1 tablespoon fresh parsley, chopped
2 tablespoons extra virgin olive oil
Salt and freshly ground black pepper, to taste
4 1-inch slices semi-stale or toasted ciabatta bread
Fresh basil leaves

Mix all the ingredients well except the bread and fresh basil leaves. Spread equal quantities of the mixture on the bread slices. Garnish with the fresh basil leaves.

Cialledda—Bread with Cucumbers and Tomatoes
4 servings

2 cups 1-inch cubes of stale bread
2 ripe tomatoes cut in 1-inch cubes
8 fresh basil leaves, thinly sliced
a pinch of oregano
1 large seeded cucumber, cut in 1-inch cubes
¼ cup extra virgin olive oil
½ cup sliced sweet Vidalia onions
dash of salt and freshly ground black pepper
dash of hot pepper seeds

Place bread cubes in a large bowl, sprinkle warm water over them and toss to make them semi-soft. Add the rest of the ingredients and mix well. Serve for lunch or a snack.

Fiore Di Latte Caprese—Sliced Mozzarella Salad
4 servings

4 containers Ovoline fresh mozzarella, each sliced in 4
2 large ripe tomatoes, cut into 16 slices
16 fresh basil leaves
¼ cup of extra virgin olive oil
sea salt and freshly ground black pepper, to taste

Arrange alternating slices of the mozzarella and to-mato on a platter. Place a basil leaf beside each tomato slice. Drizzle with olive oil. Sprinkle with salt and pepper. Serve with balsamic vinaigrette (optional).

Focaccia Bread Barese-style (called *chich* in Sannicandro Di Bari)
8 servings

For the dough:
1½ cups warm water
1 oz. dry yeast
1 teaspoon granulated sugar
2 teaspoons salt
1 tablespoon olive oil
3½ cups high-gluten all-purpose flour

To finish the dish:
Extra virgin olive oil
1 medium tomato, cut in small cubes
oregano and sea salt

To make the dough, combine the warm water and dry yeast in a mixing bowl. Set aside to rest until the dough doubles in size. Add the rest of ingredients and mix well until you have a smooth ball of dough and the sides of the bowl are clean. Place the dough on a floured surface and kneed by hand for 10 minutes. Shape it into a ball, place it in a well-oiled dish, cover and set aside to rest for 2 hours.

On a well-oiled deep-dish pizza pan, stretch the dough. Generously drizzle extra virgin olive oil to cover the dough. Using your index finger, make indentations down to the bottom of the pan, one inch apart. Place a cube of fresh tomato in each indentation. Sprinkle generously with oregano and sea salt. Set aside to rest for 30 minutes.

Preheat the oven to 400 degrees. Place the focaccia on the middle shelf and bake for 20 minutes, until golden-brown. Best eaten warm!

Pizza Sauce (also, *Amogio Sauce*)
2 cups

2 cups canned crushed tomato
2 tablespoon olive oil
1 teaspoon sugar
2 teaspoons salt
1 teaspoon granulated garlic,
½ teaspoon oregano
½ teaspoon basil
¼ teaspoon hot pepper seeds

In a mixing bowl, combine all the ingredients and whisk until the oil is evenly distributed in the sauce. Serve as *Amogio Sauce* for dipping, along with a focaccia bread dribbled with olive oil.

Panzerotti—Stuffed Pizza Pockets
8 servings

focaccia dough (see *Focaccia Bread Barese-style*, above)
oil
Pizza Sauce (see *Pizza Sauce,* above)
fresh mozzarella, cut in 1-ounce cubes
1 egg
1 teaspoon milk (approximately)

Roll and cut focaccia dough into 8 2-ounce balls. Place the balls on a tray. Lightly brush with oil set aside for one hour. In a deep frying pan, heat the oil to 300 degrees. On a floured surface, roll each ball into an 8-inch round circle. Place a teaspoon of pizza sauce in the center of each one and top with a cube of fresh mozzarella.

In a small bowl, mix the egg with a few drops of milk. Brush the mixture along the edge of each circle. Fold the circles into half-moons and pinch the edges together with a floured fork. Place the half-moons into hot oil and fry until golden brown on both sides. Remove with a slotted spoon and place on a tray lined with absorbent paper.

Enjoy while warm.

Pizza Fritta—Fried Pizza Dough
4 servings

2 3-ounce balls of *Focaccia* dough (see above), prepared
2 hours earlier
2 cups frying oil
2 tablespoons granulated sugar
1 teaspoon cinnamon

In a large frying pan, heat the oil. On a floured surface, roll each pizza ball into a thin pizza. With a pizza cutter, cut each circle into 8 triangles. Fry each triangle on both sides until golden and place on absorbent towels.

Combine the sugar and cinnamon. Generously sprinkle the mixture on both sides of the pizza triangles. Eat while warm.

Involtini Di Melanzane—Stuffed Rolled Eggplant with Ricotta
4 servings

1 large eggplant
salt
1 cup flour
2 cups Italian bread crumbs
1 egg
¼ cup heavy cream
8 ounces spinach leaves, well washed
2 cups olive oil
1 pound fresh Ricotta

1 teaspoon granulated garlic
½ cup Parmesan cheese
salt and pepper to taste

Peel and slice the eggplant lengthwise as thinly as possible. Place on a tray and sprinkle with a little salt. Set aside. Place the flour on a large plate and the bread-crumbs on another plate. Beat the egg and cream together in a bowl and set aside.

In a sauté pan, place the spinach with few drops of the oil and cook over medium heat, stirring, until soft. Do not overcook. Remove from the heat to cool. Squeeze the spinach into a ball to drain off as much liquid as possible. Place the spinach on a cutting board, chop roughly, and transfer to a mixing bowl. Add the Ricotta, garlic, Parmesan cheese, salt, and pepper. Mix well and set aside.

Rinse the eggplant slices in cold water, pat them dry, and lay them on a large kitchen surface. Divide the spinach and Ricotta mixture into equal portions, one for each slice of eggplant. Place a portion of the mixture in the center of each slice of eggplant. Gently roll up the eggplant and turn the sides inwards to seal in the mixture.

Place side by side: the flour, the egg-and-cream mixture, the bread crumbs, and a large empty tray. Roll each eggplant in the flour, dip it in the egg-and-cream mixture, roll it over the bread crumbs, and place it on the tray until all are coated. Heat the oil in a frying pan and fry until golden-brown. Serve warm with a side of marinara sauce.

Fettuccine Gabriella—Seafood Pasta
6 servings

1 pound fettuccine (Barilla)
2 6-ounce lobster tails
½ cup olive oil
12 large sea scallops
12 large shrimps, peeled and deveined
6 cloves garlic, chopped
2 ounces dry white wine
½ cup heavy cream
3 cups marinara sauce
salt and pepper to taste
2 tablespoons fresh basil, chopped

Boil the fettuccine in salted water until al dente. Drain, place into individual bowls for your guests, and set aside. Cut the lobster tails in half, extract the meat, and cut it into large cubes. In a large sauté pan, heat the oil until it is hot, add all the seafood, and stir well for 2 minutes. Add the garlic and stir well for 2 minutes until the shrimps are firm. Deglaze with wine, add the cream, and bring to a boil. Add the marinara sauce, season with the salt and pepper, and spoon over the fettuccine. Garnish with the fresh basil.

NOTE: Do not overcook the seafood to prevent it from becoming tough and rubbery.

Linguine con Aglio e Oglio—Linguine with Olive Oil and Garlic
4 servings

1 pound linguine pasta
8 cloves garlic
½ cup olive oil
2 tablespoons fresh parsley, chopped
pinch of salt and freshly ground black pepper, to taste
grated Parmesan cheese (optional)

In a large pot of salted water, boil the linguine until al dente. Drain and set aside. While the linguine is boiling, peel and chop the garlic cloves to the size you like. In a large skillet, heat the olive oil, add the garlic, and stir until golden but not brown. Add the pasta, stir frequently for 2 to 3 minutes. Add the parsley, salt and pepper, mix, and serve with a bowl of grated cheese.

Spaghetti alla Carbonara—Spaghetti Coal-Mining Style
4 servings

4 eggs
½ cup Parmigiano-Reggiano cheese
1 ounce milk
1 pound bacon, medium-sliced
1 pound spaghetti
2 tablespoons onions, chopped
6 cloves garlic, minced
1 teaspoon hot pepper seeds (optional)
2 tablespoons fresh parsley, chopped
⅓ cup olive oil

In a medium size bowl, beat the eggs, Parmigiano-Reggiano cheese, and milk. Set aside. Slice the bacon crosswise and fry it in a large skillet until it becomes lean. Drain the fat from skillet and set aside. Boil the spaghetti in salted water until it is al dente and drain.

Add the onions and garlic to the bacon and cook on low heat until the garlic is golden, but not brown. Add the spaghetti to the bacon and mix well. Add the olive oil and the egg-and-cheese mixture. Stir frequently until the egg mixture is cooked. Mix in the hot pepper seeds and parsley.

Pasta con Cavolfiore Di San Giuseppe— Rigatoni with Purple Cauliflower
8 servings

1 cup olive oil
1½ cups bread crumbs (Panko is preferred)
1 pound rigatoni (Barilla is preferred)
1 medium purple cauliflower, cut in small florets
2 large onions, thinly sliced
Black pepper, freshly ground
Parmesan cheese
½ cup fresh basil leaves, thinly sliced

In a small frying pan, add ¼ cup of the olive oil and fry the bead crumbs until crisp and golden-brown. (Fried bread crumbs are called *mollica fritta* in Italian.) Remove from the heat and set aside. In a large pot of salted water, boil the rigatoni until it is half cooked. Add the cauliflower and cook until the pasta is al dente. Drain and set aside. In a large frying pan, heat the remaining oil and fry the onions until golden-brown. Serve the pasta and cauliflower in 8 bowls and sprinkle with the bread crumbs. Drizzle a teaspoon of olive oil and spoon the onions over the pasta. Mix in the fresh ground black pepper, Parmesan cheese, and basil leaves.

NOTE: If you don't have purple cauliflower, you can substitute white cauliflower.

Salsa Di Pomodoro—Tomato Sauce
1 quart

¼ cup olive oil
1 small onion, diced
8 garlic cloves, minced
4 cups crushed tomato pulp (Roma tomatoes are preferred)
6 fresh basil leaves
1 teaspoon sugar
1 teaspoon hot red pepper seeds
salt to taste
1 cup olive oil

In a heavy saucepan, heat the ¼ cup of oil, add onions and garlic, reduce the heat, and cook until golden, but not brown. Add the tomato pulp, bring to a boil, and reduce the heat to low. Add the rest of the ingredients except the one cup of oil. Simmer for one hour. Adjust the seasoning adding more red pepper if you like hot sauce or a little more sugar if you prefer it sweeter. Remove from heat and set aside to cool for 30 minutes.

Using a wire whisk, pour the remaining cup of oil into the sauce, a little at the time while stirring continuously, until the oil is fully absorbed. This will make the sauce rich and thick.

NOTE: Use this recipe in many dishes, including the preparation of Marinara, Parmigiana, or Napolitano sauces, and in lasagna, spaghetti, or any other pasta or vegetarian dishes.

Melanzane alla Parmigiana—Eggplant Parmesan
8 servings

2 cups olive oil
4 whole eggs
½ cup milk
2 medium-size eggplants, peeled, sliced ¼ inch thick
1 cup flour
1 quart Tomato Sauce *(Salsa Di Pomodoro,* above)
4 containers Ovoline fresh mozzarella, crumbled
6 tablespoons Parmesan cheese, grated

Heat the oil in a large skillet over medium heat. In a mixing bowl, whisk the eggs and milk together. Dust the eggplant slices in the flour and then in the egg-and-milk mixture. Place them in the hot oil and fry on both sides until golden-brown. With a slotted spoon, remove the eggplant from the heat and lay on paper towels to drain. Set aside to cool.

Pre-heat the oven to 350 degrees. Spray the bottom of a deep Pyrex or oven-proof dish with food-release. Cover the bottom of the dish with a layer of pomodoro sauce. Add a layer of eggplant slices, followed by another layer of Pomodoro sauce. Sprinkle the mozzarella and Parmesan cheese over the top. Then repeat the process until the dish is full. Cover loosely with foil and bake until hot in center (approximately one hour). Remove from the oven and set aside to rest for one our before serving.

OPTION: Incorporate a layer or two of cooked penne or rigatoni pasta.

Cavatelli con Rapini—Homemade Cavatelli Pasta with Broccoli Rabe
8 servings

1 quart Five Roses flour (imported from Canada)
1 tablespoon salt
2 bunches of broccoli rabe
¼ teaspoon salt
1 cup extra virgin olive oil
8 cloves garlic, minced
salt and freshly ground black pepper
hot pepper seeds (optional)

To make the pasta dough:
Bring one quart of water to a boil and transfer to a mixing bowl. Add the salt and flour and mix until the dough comes away from the sides of mixing bowl, leaving it clean. Remove the pasta dough, place on a corner of a wooden table, and cover with plastic wrap. Leave it covered.

To make the cavatelli:
Measure 2-ounce chunks of warm dough. Use very little flour as you extend the chunks into a long, skinny, round noodles, about 12 to 14 inches long, by rubbing it on your working counter or table with both hands, starting from the center moving outwards. Repeat the process to make 5 noodles. Sprinkle the noodles with flour, cut them with a knife or table spatula into ½-inch nuggets, and sprinkle them with flour again to prevent them from

sticking together. Place two fingers on top of each nugget and push down gently, simultaneously pulling the dough towards you, until it forms a small oval shell. Place the nuggets on a well-floured tray and leave for one hour or until dry. Loosen the pieces with a spatula and leave them on the tray with space between them before cooking. To preserve for future use, transfer the nuggets to a plastic bag, seal the bag, and keep it in the freezer.

To prepare the dish:

Cut off the tough part of the broccoli rabe stems and discard. Rinse the vegetable a few times until clean and set aside. Fill a pot large enough to contain the vegetable and cavatelli three-quarters full of water, add the salt, and bring to a boil. Place the vegetable in the water, bring to a boil again, and cook for 3 minutes or until half done. Add the cavatelli and continue to boil uncovered until the pasta rises to the top of the pot and the vegetable is semi-soft. Remove the ingredients with a slotted spoon, drain, and set aside.

In a large frying pan, heat the extra virgin olive oil, add the garlic, and sauté until golden but not brown. Add the cavatelli and broccoli rabe, turn off the heat, and stir gently. Season with the salt, black pepper, and hot pepper seeds.

Chef's Favorite Recipes

Brown Sugar and Maple Panna Cotta
8 servings

1 cup water
1 envelope clear gelatin
½ cup whipping cream
½ cup light brown sugar, packed
½ dairy sour cream
½ cup whipping cream
1 teaspoon maple syrup
fresh berries of your choice
fresh mint leaves

Pour the water into a small bowl, sprinkle in the gelatin, and set aside without mixing. Place 8 6-ounce ramekins in a shallow baking pan, spray them with food release, and set aside.

In a medium saucepan, place ½ cup whipping cream and the brown sugar, and heat over medium-high but do not boil, stirring continually. When the mixture is hot, add the gelatin and water, stir well, and remove from the heat. Add the sour cream and whisk until smooth. Mix in the remaining ½ cup whipping cream and maple syrup.

Pour the mixture into the ramekins, cover the pan with plastic wrap, and refrigerate for 4 to 24 hours.

Before serving, immerse the bottom of a ramekin in hot water for 10 seconds and run a small knife around the edge of the panna cotta to loosen it. Place a dessert plate on top upside down, invert, and gently remove the ramekin so that the panna cotta rests in the middle of the plate. Repeat with the remaining ramekins. Garnish with the fresh berries and mint leaves.

Tiramisu
12 servings

12 eggs
2 cups granulated sugar
2 pounds Mascarpone cheese
36 ladyfinger biscuits (2 packages)
cocoa powder
fresh berries

Separate the egg yolks and place in the top part of a double boiler (or a medium-size stainless steel bowl). Set the whites aside in a mixing bowl. Add the granulated sugar to the yolks, place the double boiler over medium heat, and whisk the mixture to dissolve the sugar until you achieve a thick, rich, shiny consistency. Keep the water hot but not boiling, so that the egg mixture is just warm enough for the sugar to dissolve. (Too much heat will scramble the eggs!) Remove from the heat and set aside.

Whisk the egg whites until they form stiff peaks and set aside. Whisk the Mascarpone cheese into the egg yolk mixture until smooth. Using a large serving spoon or rubber spatula, gently fold the egg whites into the egg yolk-and-cheese mixture until just combined. (Do not over-stir or the mixture will not stay fluffy.) Set aside.

Dip the ladyfingers in warm espresso coffee for 5 seconds and place them side by side on the bottom of a 12x12-inch square Pyrex dish, without overlapping. Spoon half of the egg mixture over the ladyfingers and spread it evenly. Add another layer of espresso-dipped ladyfingers, followed by the remaining egg mixture. Smooth the top with a stainless steel spatula, cover with plastic wrap, and refrigerate for 4 to 24 hours.

When you are ready to serve, generously sprinkle the top with cocoa powder to cover the white surface. Cut into 12 equal portions and top with fresh berries.

Pastry Cream *(to be used in various recipes)*
Makes 2½ cups

2 cups of milk
¼ cup sugar
2 egg yolks + 1 egg
⅓ cup sugar
¼ cup corn starch
1 teaspoon vanilla extract
2 tablespoons butter

Over medium heat, bring the milk and the ¼ cup of sugar to a boil, stirring frequently to avoid scorching. In a small bowl, whisk the eggs, the ⅓ cup of sugar, and the corn starch until smooth. Pour half of the sweetened milk into the eggs, stir well, and pour the mixture back into the remaining milk. Bring to a boil, stirring frequently to avoid scorching, until the mixture thickens. Remove from heat, add the vanilla extract, and mix in the butter. Pour into a stainless steel bowl, cover with plastic wrap, punch a small hole in the plastic with a fork or knife (so the warm air can escape), and refrigerate for 4 to 24 hours.

Fresh Fruit Torte
12 servings

1 10-inch round yellow cake (made from your own recipe or a cake mix)
2 ounces grenadine syrup
2 cups pastry cream (see recipe above)
1 pint of each of black, red, and blue berries
1 ripe mango, peeled and cut in small cubes
1 quart whipping cream
4 kiwis, peeled and cut into slices
12 chocolate covered strawberries

Cut the cake horizontally through the center to make 2 even rounds. Place the bottom round on a serving tray and drizzle with the grenadine. Spread the pastry cream evenly on top, cover with half of the berries, and follow with an even layer of mango cubes. Place the top round of the cake on top and press gently.

Whisk the whipping cream until it forms a stiff peak and spread it smoothly over the cake. Arrange the kiwi slices around the outer edge of the cake, leaving 12 equidistant spots for the chocolate-covered strawberries. Place the blue berries in an even circle inside the kiwi slices, followed by a circle of the red berries and a circle of the black berries. Repeat with all the berries until the top of the cake is covered. Place the chocolate-covered strawberries around the edge of the cake between the kiwi slices. Refrigerate for 2 hours.

To serve, cut the cake into 12 portions, each with a chocolate-covered strawberry. This dessert is a family favorite.

Christmas Holiday Recipes

Vigilia Di Natale a Casa Di Beato—
Christmas Eve at the Beatos'

Our Christmas celebration is a family tradition—gathering together, feasting, arguing, getting loud, and keeping the doors open all night long because everyone was welcome. This was a holiday of love and compassion, so friends and strangers alike came to eat, and Dago Red wine flowed around the table, as we awaited the birth of the new King.

Every year, my dad made a large *presepio*, or Nativity scene. On a large wooden table, he would shape a barn with pine branches and line the back and inside walls with old paper bags once filled with cement. He would add a small, dim lightbulb and a short string of Christmas lights. At that time, we didn't have gold and silver balls, so he used fruit. In October, he would pick bunches of grapes, winter pears, and quinces on 4-inch stems and preserve them by sticking each stem into a small potato, whose juices nourished the fruit for two months, preventing dryness and decay. He would hang these fruits with the potatoes from the attic ceiling, giving us all strict orders not to touch or eat the fruit until Christmas Eve, after baby Jesus was born. Every year, this was our "forbidden fruit."

Our house was attached to a small church called Spirito Santo (Holy Spirit). Just before Mass, Father Martinelli would come in and bless the Nativity scene. Following the midnight Mass, the celebration would continue with treats like *cartellate* and hot chestnuts. After unbuckling our belts so we could breathe, the games would begin. The children sat at one end of the table with the ladies, who played Tombola (bingo). My mom would cut little pieces of orange rind to mark the numbers when they were called. The men sat at the other end of the table playing Italian card games, *Scopa*, *Briscola*, and *Tressette*. This was the highlight of the evening for my dad. We played all night until we were so tired that we were falling asleep. There was never an exchange of gifts among the adults, and the children waited until the "Epiphany of Our Lord" on January 7 to receive a gift.

On Christmas Day, after the 12 o'clock Mass, we would eat dinner. My mom would prepare meat, usually stuffed rabbit, with baked potatoes, which was served after a big plate of pasta with tomato sauce that had been simmering since 8:00 a.m. It was customary for the children to secretly buy a Christmas card, usually with a religious scene outside and blank inside. Each of us would write a poem we had learned in school and place the card under one of my parents' dishes so when they cleared the table it would be a surprise. We would then stand up and recite the poem in front of everybody. In return, our parents gave us money, a gift we had earned for Christmas.

New Year's Eve was not a big deal. We played the same games that we had played on Christmas. Veal was our traditional specialty dish. We stayed up until midnight and rang in the new year with a bottle of Spumante. On New Year's Day, after church, we ate pasta and meat, usually sausage, cooked over coals.

Tradition says that on January 6, the three Wise Men arrived at the manger where Jesus was born, to visit and bring gifts. On this day, the children in our family received gifts from the Befana, who we called Strega Nona (not Santa Claus) after the story by Tomie de Paola. Children believed that a witch flew on a broom through a chimney, bringing stockings full of candies and little toys— with charcoal mixed in if they were bad. My home town, Sannicandro, had one large crossroad. In the center was a 30-foot Christmas tree, which was lit up and roped off during the holidays. On the day of the Epiphany, the city would put about a hundred well-wrapped gifts around the tree, and the mayor would invite a hundred kids from poor families to receive a gift, as large crowds watched. This event concluded the Christmas holidays.

On the following pages you will find our traditional Christmas holiday recipes.

Mafalda con Acciughe—Curly Wide Noodles with Anchovies
20 servings

4 pounds mafalda noodles
6 ounces canned anchovies
2 cups extra virgin olive oil
salt and freshly ground black pepper or hot pepper seeds

In a large pot, bring salted water to boil, add the noodles, and cook until they are al dente. Drain and set aside. In a large skillet, heat the olive oil, add the anchovies, and stir for a second. Quickly add the drained pasta, remove from the heat, and mix well. Add the seasoning.

For children and non-anchovy lovers, retain some of the drained pasta and serve with Pomodoro Sauce (see recipe above).

NOTE: This dish is served as a first course. All the others are placed on the table to be enjoyed during the all-night feast.

Insalata Di Polpo—Octopus Salad
20 servings

24 pounds frozen medium-size octopus, imported from
Spain or Italy
2 cups celery, diced
1 cup fresh parsley, chopped
12 garlic cloves, thinly sliced
salt and freshly ground black pepper
1 cup extra virgin olive oil

Bring a large pot of salted water to a boil, add the octopus, reduce the heat, and simmer (to avoid shrinkage) for 3 to 4 hours or until tender. Place the pot under the faucet and run cold water into it. (This will enable you to work easily with your hands.) While the water is running over the octopus, strip the tentacles and suction cups off of the skin and rinse well. Cut into pieces ½-inch thick and place them in large bowl. Add the celery, parsley, garlic, salt, black pepper, and olive oil. Mix thoroughly.

NOTE: Mix in the olive oil just before serving. Adding it too soon and refrigerating will make the dish heavy and greasy.

Baccalá Frito—Fried Salted Cod
24 servings

6 pounds dried salted cod *(baccalá)*
flour
3 cups olive oil

Four or five days before you serve this dish, place the cod in a large container of cold water with at least 2 inches above the top of the fish and refrigerate. Drain and change the water twice daily so the cod becomes soft and puffy. A few hours before dinner, place the flour in a mixing bowl. Cut the cod in to 3-inch pieces, coat them in the flour, and fry in olive for 3 to 4 minutes on each side, until golden brown. Remove with a slotted spoon and drain on absorbent paper before serving. Serve at room temperature.

Calzone Di Cipolla—Onion Pie
16 servings

2 balls focaccia dough, 1 pound each
20 bunches green onions, trimmed, washed, and cut into 1-inch pieces
20 pitted Kalamata olives, halved
12 cherry tomatoes, quartered
1 cup extra virgin olive oil
salt and freshly ground black pepper, to taste
1 tablespoon granulated garlic
12 anchovies, chopped (optional)

Prepare the focaccia dough (see *Focaccia Bread Barese-style*, above).

In a large pot, bring salted water to a boil and add the onions. Push the onions down with a skimmer or slotted spoon to keep them continuously submerged. Boil for 5 minutes, until semi-tender—neither hard nor mushy. Do not decrease the heat. Drain into a large colander, and place the onions under cold running water to cool. Press the onions down with the palm of your hand to squeeze out all the water. Set the colander on a tray for 2 hours or refrigerate overnight to extract any excess water (this step is very important).

Turn the onions into a large bowl. Add the olives, tomatoes, olive oil, salt, pepper, and garlic. Mix gently. Add the chopped anchovies.

Preheat the oven to 390 degrees. Place one dough ball of focaccia dough on a well-floured kitchen surface. Using a rolling pin, stretch the dough into a 24-inch round. Oil the bottom and sides of a 16-inch deep dish pizza pan and place the rolled-out dough into it. Allow the excess dough to hang over the sides of the dish. Place the onion mixture over the dough and spread evenly. Roll out the second dough ball until it is a 24-inch round and place it over the onions to seal the pie. Using a hard spatula or knife, press the dough around edge of the dish. Cut off the excess dough, cringe and folding inwards so the edges of the top and bottom pastries are sealed. Generously brush the top of the pie with olive oil, as well as the edges. Make a 1-inch cut in the center of the top crust of the pie.

Bake for 45 minutes or until the crust is golden brown on the top and bottom. Remove from the oven and set aside to cool.

Lots of patience and love goes into this family favorite. I don't remember a Christmas eve without a *calzone*. Enjoy!

Fritto Misto—Assorted Fried Fish Country-Style
12 servings

perch, tilapia, salmon, flounder (12 1-ounce pieces of each)
3 cups flour
4 eggs
1 cup milk
3 cups olive oil
12 lemon slices

Cut all the fish in 1-inch slices. Beat the milk and eggs for 3 minutes, until well incorporated.

Dust each piece of fish in the flour, dip it in the egg mixture, and fry in hot oil until golden brown. Remove with a slotted spoon and drain on absorbent paper. Arrange on platter with the lemons slices.

Calamari Fritti—Fried Calamari
12 servings

3 pounds calamari, cleaned, rinsed, and sliced
¼ cup salt
2 cups flour
olive oil

Put the calamari into a large bowl, sprinkle the ¼ cup salt over it, and mix until the salt dissolves. Place the calamari in a strainer until the liquid is well drained. In a deep frying pan, heat the oil to 300 degrees. Dust the calamari in the flour and fry one cup at a time until crisp. Drain briefly on absorbent paper and serve hot.

Vincotto—Fig and Wine Syrup
4 cups

12 dry figs
2 bottles Cabernet or Primitivo Dago Red wine
1 large orange
1 cup of sugar

Cut away the hard fig stems and discard. Dice the figs. Remove the rind from the orange. Place the figs, orange rind, wine, and sugar in a heavy pot, bring to a boil, reduce to simmer, and cook for 3 hours or until the quantity is reduced to half. Remove from the heat and set aside for 30 minutes.

Remove the orange rind and discard it. Pour the mixture into a blender or food processor (do not use an electric mixer) and mix until you have a thick, smooth consistency. Strain the through a fine strainer or cheese cloth.

NOTE: Vincotto can be prepared and refrigerated in a closed container for up to 12 months.

Cartellate Natalizie Barese in Vincotto— **Christmas Pastries**
24 pastries

3 cups vincotto (recipe above)
4 cups flour, sifted
1 egg
3 tablespoons olive oil
1 cup white wine, room temperature
pinch of salt
canola oil for deep-frying

Make the *vincotto* first and set aside (see the previous recipe), or use your prepared *vincotto* if you made it ahead of time.

To make the cartellate:
Place the flour on a working surface and make a 6-inch well in the center. In a mixing bowl, beat the egg and add the 3 tablespoons of oil, the wine, and the salt. Combine thoroughly and pour the wet mixture into the center of the well. Use your fingers to mix a little of the flour at the time into the liquid until you have a smooth ball of dough. If it is sticky, mix in a little more flour. Knead the

dough for 10 minutes, cover with plastic wrap, and set aside for 20 minutes.

Cut away a quarter of the dough and roll out a thin sheet with a rolling pin. Using a stainless steel crinkle cut knife, divide the sheet into 2x12-inch strips, about the size of a ruler. Shape the pastry by pinching the dough along the outside edge of one strip, leaving about 2 inches between each pinch. This should form little pockets or bows, which will later contain some of your fig-and-wine syrup *(vincotto)*. Turn the strip to form a wheel and pinch together the dough on the inside of the bows so they hold their shape. Lift the pastry strip with a flat spatula and place on a floured tray. Repeat with all the strips. Set aside to dry for one hour.

In a large pan, pour the frying oil to a depth of 3 inches and heat to 300 degrees. Using a flat spatula, lower the pastry strips into the oil and fry, flipping them over until golden-brown. Remove from the oil with a slotted spoon and drain on absorbent paper until cool enough to handle with your fingers.

Before serving:

Heat the vincotto in a deep pan until it simmers. One at a time, dip the cartellate pastries into the syrup for few seconds, remove, and place on a serving tray, making sure the bows are semi-filled with liquid. Loosely cover with a clean, dry cloth and keep in cool, dry place until it is time to serve. Sprinkle with ground cinnamon and clove.

NOTE: Cartellate can be made up to a week before serving and refrigerate. This is another dish prepared with a lot of love. Christmas Eve cannot be celebrated without it.

Side Dishes

Castagne Arrostite—Roasted Chestnuts
5 pounds chestnuts

Using a small knife on the flat top of each chestnut, cut a small cross through the skin, without piercing the flesh of the nut. Arrange the chestnuts on a perforated steel pan. Cook the chestnuts over hot coals or in an oven, as described below.

Place the pan on a rack 10 inches above live coals (without flames). Cover the pan with a heavy damp cloth. After five minutes, remove the cloth, use a flat spatula to stir and flip the chestnuts, and replace the damp cloth over the chestnuts. Repeat every few minutes for 45 minutes, stirring frequently or until the chestnuts are tender. Whenever the cloth becomes dry, dampen it by sprinkling it with water.

If you are using an oven, preheat it to 400 degrees and place the steal pan inside. Bake, stirring occasionally, for 45 minutes or until tender.

Cold Side Dishes

- ❀ **Platter of Assorted Raw Greens** (celery, fennel, green onions, and chicory)
- ❀ **Plate of Assorted Olives**
- ❀ **Platter of Assorted Nuts**
- ❀ **Whole Fruit Bowl**

Epilogue

I wrote this book to portray different aspects of my life, including people I have met and various parts of the world I traveled to.

As a young person, I lived in a town that had been dilapidated by the bombings of World War II. There were many places where we were not allowed to play because they were too dangerous, with half-destroyed buildings that took decades to demolish or rebuild. The sanitary conditions were very poor. There was no running water and toilet tissue was non-existent except in hotels and the homes of the wealthy. Stray dogs roamed through the town, suffering from starvation. Many of us had to resort to stealing food from farms, such as olives, almonds, fruit, and fresh vegetables, which we would bring home to eat. In order for my parents to buy us new shoes or a new suit for a special event, such as First Communion, Easter, or any other holiday, one of us would take their turn each year. My parents would borrow the money needed for the purchase using a payment plan, extending some of my grandparents' monthly pension as collateral, because that was the only assured income in the family.

I never realized that Italy was the most beautiful country in the world. Only in school did I learn of the historic and beautiful places, but never ventured outside our region, because we could not afford to travel. It was only when I returned home on my honeymoon with the help of the American dollar that Judy and I explored the most fantastic places, which added to the memories of my childhood of my beautiful homeland, Italy.

Switzerland, though so close to Italy, was a different world. They had not participated in any wars. The homes were old but intact, and many had balconies decorated with flowers. All the land was well-kept and practically manicured. The beautiful mountains always had some snow at the top, making them so picturesque that you felt you could almost touch from a distance. The sanitary conditions where excellent. The people were extremely friendly and generous. Switzerland gave me a chance to grow up on my own, without my parents; to make many decisions that shaped me into an adult; and, most of all, to break the hold and travel to Canada. For that, I am most indebted to Switzerland and the Swiss people.

Canada was not only the country where my career as a chef took hold, but also the land that gave me the opportunities that formed a strong foundation for my entire future. Canada was the country that gave me the chance to bring my family closer to the dream of reconciliation, which finally culminated in meeting Grandma in America. It was in Windsor that I learned English—the key to my success and independence. I developed a love for ice hockey; my favorite team was the Toronto Maple Leafs, and the Montreal Canadiens were second. In 1967, Canada celebrated a centennial, and the Stanley Cup was at center stage in the playoff finals between the competing

Maple Leafs and Canadians. A huge centennial dome was built in Montreal, where it was expected that Montreal's better team would take the Cup—but the Maple Leafs won the series four games to two and lifted the Cup.

I took interest in many other things Canadian, such as the law of the land and its political system. I admired Pierre Elliott Trudeau when he became prime minister, a man with great charisma and vision. I believed that the more informed I was, the better my decisions would be. I viewed knowledge as wealth. I became a Canadian citizen, not because I had to, but because I wanted to. I believed that if you make a living in any country you have to become part of the system. I could recite the national anthem in French and English. In Windsor I learned to drive an automobile, and that is where I got my first car, an Ambassador made by American Motors. Little did I know at the time how much I would be influenced by all the activities happening across the Detroit River.

The first time I attended a baseball game at Detroit's Tiger Stadium, the owner of a produce company had given me two free tickets. I didn't know anything about baseball, but I took the tickets and invited my girlfriend, Judy, to come with me. In the first inning, one of the players hit the ball and dropped the bat, running. I said to Judy, "Why did he drop the stick?" She laughed, and for the rest of the game, she explained what was happening play by play. At about the seventh inning I fell asleep. At the end of that season, the same guy who had given me the tickets asked if I was willing to bet twenty dollars on one of the World Series games between the Detroit Tigers and the St. Louis Cardinals. I said, "I take Detroit, and I will raise you another twenty dollars that Detroit will go all the way and win the World Series." He replied, "Game on!" I don't know why I made that bet. Saint Louis was the favorite to win, and I new little about the game. Not only did Detroit win that game, but they also won the World Series!

From the distance I watched Detroit burn. I read about the assassination of Bobby Kennedy and Martin Luther King, the Vietnam War, the protest in the streets, as the rest of the world watched and criticized. I became annoyed by all the cheap shots taken at America, by the world, including Canada, the very country whose safety America had secured in the past and was willing to do in the future. I also respected the right of free speech that Canada upheld.

* * *

America, home of the free and the brave!

After 40 plus years of being an American citizen I can say for certain that all the struggle and the time waiting to come to this country was well worth it! And the fact that I came here legally adds even more to my achievement. Detroit was the capital murder city of the nation when I got my visa, and my Canadians friends, thought I was crazy to move to Detroit. But I did it because I had ambition and was chasing a dream that Canada was perhaps not quite fulfilling. I like to tell my granddaughters, "If you have a dream, pursue it." There is nothing in this great country to hold you back from becoming whatever you want to be.

The key to success is setting your goals and working hard to achieve them. You may experience bumps and difficulties, and sometimes you will feel like giving up, but when you think that you have exhausted all avenues, try again and again until you achieve your goal. Respect the laws of the land, be a productive individual, never forget the importance of family, and be dependent on no one. Learn as much as possible about the government and the political system. Love the country but keep some fear and skepticism of the government. Remember that knowledge is wealth, and that a better-informed person makes better decisions in life.

Don't be afraid of setbacks or failing, for these are learning experiences. If you never fail, you won't know success. Don't be afraid of taking chances in life, working for yourself or somebody else. If you fail, you will know what to do next time. Remember that you live in the greatest country in the world.

It saddens me to hear many people saying that America is the problem, that America is unjust. This country has always defended freedom. It was founded on the principles that the right to live free comes from God and not from man, and that right to the pursuit of happiness is equal for everybody. America knows what freedom and tyranny are. They fought many battles to free themselves from the tyranny of the Crown of England, and many other wars to free other nations from tyranny. They also are the most charitable people in the world and always stand for human rights. There is a good reason that people from all over the world want to come here. God always blessed and will continue to bless this great country, for there is no other like it.

This book is dedicated to my parents, to all the other people who helped me achieve my dream, and to the best country in the world that gave me the opportunity to raise my wonderful family with no regrets. Thank you, America, and may God continue to bless you.

* * *

Let me leave you with couple of my favorite quotes from three American presidents. In memory of our veterans of all wars.

"Let every nation know, whether it wishes us well or ill, that we shall pay any price, bear any burden, meet any hardship, support any friend, oppose any foe to assure the survival and the success of liberty."
—John F. Kennedy (January 20, 1961, Inaugural Address, Washington, DC)

"If we ever forget that we're one nation under God, then we will be a nation gone under."
—Ronald Wilson Reagan (August 23, 1984, Ecumenical Prayer Breakfast, Dallas, Texas)

"We will not waver; we will not tire; we will not falter; and we will not fail. Peace and freedom will prevail."
—George W. Bush (October 7, 2001, Address to the Nation, Washington, DC)

Made in the USA
Lexington, KY
13 April 2016